# Romantic Getaways in the Pacific Northwest and Western Canada

Other books in the *Romantic Getaways* Series:

*Romantic Weekend Getaways: The Mid-Atlantic States, Second Edition*

*Romantic California Getaways*

*Romantic Hawaiian Getaways*

*Romantic Island Getaways*

# Romantic Getaways in the Pacific Northwest and Western Canada

LARRY FOX
BARBARA RADIN-FOX

**John Wiley & Sons, Inc.**
New York ♠ Chichester ♠ Brisbane ♠ Toronto ♠ Singapore

In recognition of the importance of preserving what has been written, it is a policy of John Wiley & Sons, Inc., to have books of enduring value published in the United States printed on acid-free paper, and we exert our best efforts to that end.

Library of Congress Cataloging in Publication Data

Fox, Larry, 1945–
    Romantic Getaways in the Pacific Northwest and Western
Canada / Larry Fox and Barbara Radin-Fox.
      p.    cm.
    Includes index.
    ISBN 0-471-53997-X
    1. Northwest, Pacific—Tours.   2. British Columbia—Tours.
I. Radin-Fox, Barbara.   II. Title.
F852.3.M66  1992
917.9504'43—dc20                        92-7197

Printed in the United States of America

10 9 8 7 6 5 4 3 2

*To each other.*
*The road has not always been easy,*
*but love kept us from getting lost.*

# Contents

# Introduction

*R*omantic Getaways in the Pacific Northwest guides you on journeys centered around specific themes. These journeys can be a getaway for a long weekend or a vacation lasting several weeks. The area we cover includes Oregon, Washington, and Alaska, as well as British Columbia and western Alberta.

Our chapters explore the very special places in the Pacific Northwest: the wine country of Washington and Oregon, the big cities, mountains and parks, scenic tours, the last frontier in Alaska, the inns and hotels where you can help detect a murderer or learn to ride a horse, outfitters who will take you on the adventure of your life, and the top annual festivals. At the end of each chapter, you'll find intimate inns, fine restaurants, and helpful telephone numbers.

We've selected these particular places because we found them exceptional in beauty, quality, location, or atmosphere. This means we have left out some familiar places—big hotels, famous but unimaginative restaurants, and ordinary museums—because we did not find them conducive to romance.

Our guide assumes that, with the exception of the big cities and much of Alaska, you will be traveling by car. Before you go, here are a few tips to make your travel easier:

🌲 Get a good map of the state and the region you are visiting. The tourist offices we list can help provide you with the maps and other information, such as exact dates and times of festivals. For more detailed information, contact the various visitors' centers listed in the chapters.

🌲 Some of the attractions listed charge a small admission price. We do not list prices that are reasonable and unexceptional because they may change before you read this. We do note admission prices if they are unusually high.

♠ Planning is the key to making your trip successful. If you have your heart set on a special tour, hike, or wilderness adventure, make reservations before you go. Many of these special trips and tours are sold out months in advance. Inns and bed and breakfasts are also booked weeks (in some cases months) ahead of time during the prime summer months. *Always* make your reservations early if you want to stay at a specific inn or hotel. Reservations are usually required at the better restaurants (although you can almost always wait to make them closer to your trip).

♠ Smokers are no longer popular guests in many small inns. If you are a smoker, ask about the rules of the house. Some inns may prefer you stay elsewhere.

♠ You may have to choose between a shared bath or a private bath at some of the inns. If sharing a bath is a potential problem, be certain the innkeeper knows that you want only a room with a private bath and, if you are sending in a deposit, be sure to get it in writing.

♠ We selected restaurants on the basis of their dinner menus. Lunch menus and prices may differ significantly. In almost every case, dress is casual—reflecting the less formal lifestyle in this region, rather than the quality of particular restaurants.

♠ Exciting nightlife, particularly good places for romantic dancing, is hard to find in smaller communities. We spent countless hours looking for just such places. In this guide, sections on nightlife are in the major cities, although exceptional nightspots in smaller communities will be mentioned.

The inns, hotels, restaurants, and attractions we have selected have warmed our hearts, and we hope you will enjoy them as we did. But before you go, remember that romance is not a destination; it is that undefinable something that you have in your heart long before you begin to plan and pack for a trip.

The trips offered here, however, can help both of you unlock that mystery and wonder.

Larry Fox
Barbara Radin-Fox

A sightseeing boat tours Maligne Lake in Jasper National Park.
*(Photograph courtesy of Alberta Tourism)*

CHAPTER 1

# Wonders of the Pacific Northwest

*N*ature's agonies and ecstasies have reigned for centuries in the Pacific Northwest. The region is a place of unsurpassed beauty and sharp contrasts: rain forests and arid deserts, frozen tundra and thermal pools, teeming city streets and wilderness where bears and eagles outnumber people, peaceful mountain peaks and summits trembling with danger, rampaging rivers and frozen waterfalls. This manifestation of nature in all its grandeur and power can often be overwhelming.

The Pacific Northwest is about the size of Western Europe— a bit more than a million square miles—with only ten-million residents. Anyone, even the least adventurous explorer, can easily leave the crush of civilization behind and enter a world whose rules are set by nature and whose land was shaped by water, fire, and ice over millions of years.

Oregon, Washington, Alaska, and the Canadian provinces of British Columbia and Alberta possess dramatic scenery and special destinations that symbolize everything that is wonderful about the region. The Very Special Places of the Pacific Northwest are Ashland, the center of cultural life in south-central Washington; Glacier Bay in southeast Alaska, a living laboratory on the ice age; Jasper and Banff National Parks in Alberta, the essence of natural beauty; Port Townsend, a Victorian seaport on the Olympic Peninsula; the Islands of Puget Sound; and Victoria, a bit of Old England in British Columbia.

These exciting places can be part of a much longer journey or just a one-destination getaway. Whichever way you include these places in your journey, there will come a point when the two of you feel that this region is the most exciting place on earth.

## *Ashland, Oregon*

Sheltered by the thickly forested Siskiyou foothills, this charming town of 15,000 in the Rogue River Valley is the heart of culture in southern Oregon.

Ashland is home to the Shakespeare Festival, a theatrical event that began in 1935 as a July 4th celebration but has now grown to encompasss three stages and lasts from February through October. Three of the Bard's plays are performed outdoors during the summer months, while contemporary plays are offered indoors at the nearby Black Swan Theater and Angus Bowmer Theater.

The outdoor stage is located in Ashland's 99-acre Lithia Park, named after the mineral springs that gush forth from the fountains there. The outdoor stage is a copy of the famed Fortune Theater in London. During the summer months, dancers, actors, and musicians dressed in Elizabethan costumes entertain theatergoers before the performances in the theater courtyard.

The Elizabethan spirit even affects the town, where some shops sport an Old English theme. During the Shakespeare play series, other activities—lectures, backstage tours, dances—are held in town. The Shakespeare Art Museum at 460 B Street displays costumes (you can even try some on) and exhibits for current productions.

Ashland also evokes memories of other cultures. The Railroad District along A Street displays some fine turn-of-the-century buildings, and Lithia Park has lovely Japanese gardens, duck ponds, hiking and biking trails, and playgrounds.

Ashland also has two wineries that are pleasant places to stop: Ashland Vineyards, at 2775 East Main Street, right in town, and Weisinger's of Ashland, at 3150 Siskiyou Boulevard, to the south. Both welcome visitors.

Ashland, a five-hour drive south of Portland on I-5, is close to the Rogue River and its whitewater diversions. During the winter, skiers flock to Mount Ashland, a 7,533-foot peak 18 miles southwest of town.

Another popular destination nearby is Jacksonville, a historic gold rush town founded in the boom in 1852. Jacksonville, about 30 miles northwest of Ashland, was a bawdy and thriving mining town in the 1850s and 1860s. About one hundred of the town's historic balustraded brick and wooden structures from that era have been restored.

California Street is home to many of these historic buildings, some of which have been converted into arts and craft galleries. Among the prominent reminders of the Gold Rush era are the Beekman House, at 325 East California Street, and the Beekman Bank, at California and Third Streets. Both were owned by Cornelius C. Beekman, the town's Wells Fargo agent and banker. Beekman's bank prospered during the gold boom in the 1860s and 1870s, but closed in 1891 after he died. The bank's furnishings date to 1863 and include the gold dust scales used during the boom years.

The McCully House at Fifth and California streets is another home from that era. Built in 1860 and recently restored, the McCully House is furnished with nineteenth-century antiques. It is open from 10:00 AM to 5:00 PM daily in July and August.

The Jacksonville Museum of Southern Oregon History, in the nineteenth-century county courthouse at 206 North Fifth Street, is another interesting attraction. The museum displays relics, clothing, toys, and other artifacts relating to pioneer life in southern Oregon. The museum, as well as the U.S. National Bank on Main Street, has maps outlining walking tours of the historic district.

Jacksonville's major event each year is the Peter Britt Music Festival, which features classical, bluegrass, jazz, dance, and other musical productions in an amphitheater formed by the hillside in the Britt Gardens on First Street south of California Street. The festival is named after Peter Britt, a Swiss immigrant who was one of Jacksonville's first settlers, a pioneer photographer, and a horticulturist whose magnificent gardens are still a wonder. His cameras and photographic equipment are on display in the history museum. The festival is held from late June through August every year.

## *Glacier Bay, Alaska*

"White Thunder" is what the Tlingit Indians called the booming, explosive sound made when large chunks of a glacier break off and fall into the water, creating an instant iceberg often larger than a house. This breathtaking act of nature is just one of the fantastic attractions in Glacier Bay National Park in Southeast Alaska.

Unlike most of the natural wonders in the Pacific Northwest, Glacier Bay is a relatively new body of water. In 1794, when Captain George Vancouver was mapping this region, the area was covered by a glacier thousands of feet thick and several miles wide. Since then, the ice has receded more than 60 miles, exposing thousands of acres of land and creating a broad bay with many inlets.

Glacier Bay National Park is a living laboratory demonstrating the effects of glaciers on the land. An estimated 16 glaciers flow in the 3.2-million-acre park, creating sensational sights and sounds. The rivers of ice seem not to move, yet the glaciers give off constant noisy groans and rumbles, small avalanches, and, occasionally, explode with sound when an enormous block of ice breaks off.

The colors of glaciers are also unusual. Some are an eerie blue often called glacier blue, while others appear cloudy and dirty because the ice is filled with soil and small rocks the glacier picked up in its passage from the mountains to the sea.

No matter what the weather is at the southern mouth of the bay, the weather close to the glaciers remains constant: drizzling, freezing, and low-lying clouds—all an effect from the huge rivers of ice.

In such a foreboding place, it is surprising to find an abundance of life. Bears, squirrels, and other small mammals are all around the bay, attracted by the large stands of willow, aspen, spruce, and hemlock that took root after the glacier ice shrank. Closer to the glaciers, the smaller ice floes are home to many frolicking sea lions that are lovable even from far away. Gulls, terns, cormorants, puffins, and other birds have colonies on the cliffs near the glaciers, attracted by the small fish and shrimp killed when ice breaks off and plunges into the bay.

Glacier Bay is reachable only by airplane, cruise ship, tour boat, or kayak. The prime visiting time is late May through September. Visitors can fly from Juneau into Gustavus, the small village near Bartlett Cove on the south end of the park. The National Park Service has a lodge there, and rangers offer nature walks, slide shows, and boat tours to see the glaciers or watch the whales, and other activities.

## Jasper and Banff

Take two fairytale mountain settings, add breathtaking scenery, crystal clear lakes, flower-filled alpine meadows, famous lodges and hotels, and an abundance of year-round recreation and you have two of Canada's finest national parks—Jasper and Banff.

Jasper National Park, located 222 miles west of Edmonton on Alberta's border with British Columbia, was created in 1907 and now covers some 4,200 square miles in the Canadian Rockies. The park, open year-round, is nature's wonderland, filled with waterfalls, lakes, glaciers, canyons, wilderness areas, wild rivers, and wild animals, including moose, elk, deer, grizzly and black bear, bighorn sheep, cougars, lynx, and wolverines.

Visiting these sights requires a lot of driving and hiking, and most visitors use Jasper, a modern resort town, as the place to stay while making daily tours of the countryside.

The park scenery is fantastic. Major attractions include the Maligne Lake, the park's largest lake, where you can take a boat tour, and Maligne Canyon, an eerie wonderland with frozen waterfalls. Park officials lead canyon tours. Both the lake and canyon are about 30 miles east of Jasper via the Maligne Road.

Five miles south of town is the Jasper Tramway (take the Whistlers Mountain exit off the Jasper-Banff Highway). The 30-passenger aerial car takes visitors up 1 1/4 miles to the 8,104-foot summit of The Whistlers. There you will find a vast alpine tundra with hiking trails, a visitors' center, and spectacular views.

# PREPARING FOR THE WEATHER

The climate of all of the coastal regions of the Pacific Northwest is uniformly mild. It is unusual to have 80-degree days in the summer or freezing temperatures or snow in the winter. No matter what season, however, nights are often chilly, even in midsummer. Most of the rain is concentrated in the months of October to the end of March. Seattle gets a lot of ribbing for its annual rainfall (which is actually less than New York's or Chicago's), but southeast Alaska and the Pacific coast of the Olympic Peninsula get far more precipitation. These regions have recorded more than 150 inches of rain a year, more than four times Seattle's measurement. The rainfall in southeastern Alaska is greater than that recorded in the rest of Alaska. Annual amounts of 5 to 15 inches are common outside of that "tail" of Alaska. There is one blessing to the rainfall: it creates the massive glaciers found in Glacier Bay and western Canada.

The climate outside of the Pacific coastal region, on the eastern side of the Rockies and Cascades, is quite different: here near-desert conditions prevail with very little rainfall and much higher temperatures in the summertime.

Temperatures in Alaska vary greatly, with the difference due more to location than to the season. Southeastern Alaska, where most tourists visit, is mild, with summer readings ranging from around 40° F to the upper 60s, and winter temperatures ranging from the 20s to low 30s. In Fairbanks and the interior, summer readings range from 50 to 70° F and winter marks from −22 to a high around −10° F. In Anchorage, summer readings are in the 50 to 65° range while winter temperatures are from below zero to the 20s.

One of the park's most popular sights is Angel Glacier on Mount Edith Cavell, reached by driving 18 miles south on Highway 93A and taking the 93A Access Road (open only from June through September). The glacier lies on the southeast face of the 11,050-foot mountain and sends a curl of ice over the face of the mountain. Hiking trails lead up to this glacial outcropping and Cavell Meadows.

Thirty miles northeast of Jasper are the Miette Hot Springs, whose warm mineral pools are open to bathers from late May through the summer.

While you can do much exploring on your own, you can also go on a group hike, which park rangers lead to a number of attractions. Pick up a schedule at the Park Information Centre in Jasper (call 403/852–6176), at the Columbia Icefields (summer only), or at the Jasper Chamber of Commerce at 632 Connaught Drive.

In the winter, skiers head to the Marmot Basin, Jasper's downhill ski area. For cross-country ski enthusiasts, the park has many miles of trails through the scenic landscape.

Jasper National Park and the adjacent 2,560-square-mile Banff National Park are connected with a magnificent highway called the Icefields Parkway. The 142-mile-long road is one of the most scenic roads in North America, passing through a landscape that combines fantastic mountain scenery with alpine meadows, glaciers, and icefields.

The highway's major attractions include the Athabasca Falls, located 19 miles south of Jasper; the Goat Lookout, a parking area offering a panoramic view of the valley, located 24 miles south of Jasper; the Sunwapta Falls, a spectacular cascade with a right-angle bend, located 33 miles south of Jasper; the Stutfield Glacier Viewpoint, located 59 miles south of Jasper; and the Columbia Icefield, a 135-square-mile icecap that is the source of the Athabasca, Saskatchewan, and Columbia glaciers.

The Athabasca and Dome glaciers can be seen from the parkway. A more comprehensive view of the icefields can be found at the Interpretive and Information Centre, which displays a scale model of the icefields and presents audio-visual shows and other exhibits. The Centre is open from 9:00 AM to 5:00 PM daily from late May to mid-June; 9:00 AM to 7:00 PM from mid-June to Labor Day; and 9:00 AM to 5:00 PM again until Thanksgiving, when the center closes for the winter. Snowcoach tours and glacier hikes are offered from May through September.

The Icefields Parkway continues southeast, passing through scenery that is constantly captivating, and then reaches three-mile-long Lake Louise, 138 miles south of Jasper. This magnificent setting, next to 10,000-foot peaks in the Canadian Rockies and under the dominating presence of the Victoria Glacier—an ice river almost one hundred feet thick—is spectacular. The resort offers sports activities year-round and has the cosmopolitan atmosphere of a sophisticated town. The great landmark of the town is the Chateau Lake Louise, which sits on the edge of the lovely Lake Louise.

Lake Louise, named after Queen Victoria's daughter, is the jewel of the 2,500-square-mile Banff National Park. Just outside of town, via Highway 1A, is the Continental Divide, the geological point where all waters flow either east to the Atlantic Ocean or Gulf of Mexico or west to the Pacific Ocean. Stop for a romantic meal at the picnic area and watch the geological principle in action: a creek here separates in mid-flow, with one stream heading east, the other going west.

Continue driving south for 34 miles on the Icefields Parkway until you reach Banff, the second major resort in this park. Banff is a serene alpine village, with outstanding mountain scenery, wooded valleys, clear lakes and rivers, and a host of man-made attractions.

Banff Centre on St. Julien Road is the cultural center, with splendid concerts, plays, and arts exhibitions. The Walter Phillips Gallery nearby displays a varied selection of contemporary art.

In the heart of town is the Natural History Museum, with exhibits on the biological and geological past of the Rockies. The museum is located upstairs at the Clock Tower Mall at 112 Banff Avenue. A short walk away is the Banff Park Museum at 93 Banff

Avenue—a Victorian mansion frozen in time. It displays exhibits on birds and animals of the region. Also close by at 111 Bear Street is the Whyte Museum of the Canadian Rockies, which displays mountain paintings and photography, and exhibits of regional and national art.

Take the Banff Avenue bridge across the Bow River to the Cascade Gardens, a pleasant and romantic spot adorned with gazebos, waterworks, and gardens. From this circle, take Spray Avenue to its end where you will find the stately Banff Springs Hotel, a grand resort built in 1888 that is still captivating despite its age.

In the winter, skiers head to three resorts in the park. Sunshine Village is seven miles west of Banff, and Mt. Norquay is three miles outside the resort town. The other ski area is at Lake Louise.

Before leaving Banff, take a moment to drive on Mountain Avenue 2.6 miles south to Upper Hot Springs and the bubbling sulphur pools there. You can soak in the 93–108° F waters and get a massage. Returning to town will take you past the Sulphur Mountain Gondola Lift, which leads up to an observation deck with a grand 360-degree view of Banff and the park. From this lookout, the true majesty of Banff National Park and the Canadian Rockies is revealed.

## Port Townsend

Booms that go bust often have silver linings. This port town, on a finger of land on the northeast corner of the Olympic Peninsula, was a prosperous seaport in the 1800s. In the 1890s, though, the railroad bypassed the town, ending the boom. While jobs and industry went elsewhere, the majestic Victorian homes and buildings, built in the good times on the bluff overlooking the waterfront, stayed on. Now, almost a century later, some 50 of these stately Victorians have been reborn—refurbished and repainted in their original Victorian colors and often turned into bed and breakfasts (B&Bs).

♣

# SEARCHING FOR WHALES

Whale watching is a popular pastime in the waters of the Pacific Northwest. The bountiful waters and sounds offer a haven for the thousands of gray, minke, orcas and other species of whales that migrate in these waters every year.

When should you look for the whales? The gray whales visit these waters from March to May, while the Orcas and other species live here year-round. Go in the morning when the waters are calm and look for a whale blow—the vapor, water, or condensation that spouts in the air when the whale exhales. Binoculars will help you spot the giant mammals.

The nation's official whale-watching park, Lime Kiln State Park, is six miles west of the seaport of Friday Harbor on San Juan Island. While on the island you may also wish to stop by the Whale Museum, at 62 1st Street North in Friday Harbor. The small museum has interesting and informative displays of whale models, skeletons, and videos. Another prime whale-watching location is the Long Beach Peninsula on Washington's southwestern coast. You can take a cruise on a boat to look at the whales close-up in the sound. The Rosario Princess conducts whale-watching and other nature cruises on an 83-foot boat that sails out of Bellingham. Call 206/734–8866.

Port Townsend is reachable by ferry from Whidbey Island or by car via I-5 and Highway 101 north. If you drive, stop by the visitors' center on Highway 20 as you enter the town and pick up a map to the main attractions.

Start a tour with a walk down Water Street, which is home to many brick Victorian houses. Here you will also find the Captain's Gallery, with a nice array of kaleidoscopes; the Baltic Art Gallery, which sells ceramics and other works of art; and Earthworks, which sells ceramics.

On the Oregon coast, the best places to watch for whales in the winter are at Cape Mears State Park and Depoe Bay. In the winter, whale-watching boats depart from Depoe Bay. In the spring, Cape Arago State Park and Port Orford Heads State Wayside are also good whale-spotting places.

In Canada, the small towns of Ucluelet and Tofino on the western shore of Vancouver Island are considered the whale-watching capitals of Canada. Twenty thousand gray whales pass by each year during March through May on their way to the Bering Sea.

Whale-watching trips may be booked through Ocean Pacific Whale Charters Ltd., Box 590, Tofino, BC V0R 2Z0. 604/725–3919; Sea Smoke Sailing Charter & Tours, Box 483, Alert Bay, BC V0N 1A0. 604/974–5225; and Stubbs Island Charters, whose whale-watching ships sail from Telegraph Cove, about ten miles south of Port McNeill. Call 604/974–5403.

In Alaska, whale-watching tours cruise the Inside Passage, passing Ketchikan and Juneau on the way. A tour ship, Bendixen Yacht, cruises the intricate waterways of the Inland Passage so that passengers may see whales, bald eagles, and glaciers as well as go fishing. Contact them at P.O. Box 210835-AK, Auke Bay, AK 99821 or 818-AK W Argand, Seattle, WA 98119. 206/285–5999.

The finest mansion in town is the Ann Starrett Mansion, a superb home with an octagonal tower with gabled wings. It's at 744 Clay Street and is now a bed-and-breakfast inn. Another Victorian B&B with great views is the James House, at 1238 Washington Street. Other fine homes include the Bartlett House at the end of Polk Street and the Daniel Logan House at Lawrence and Taylor streets.

Several public buildings are open for tours. The City Hall, a remarkable building with touches of Gothic, Romanesque, and whimsical in its design, at Water and Madison streets, has a nice museum with Victorian artifacts. The Rothschild House at Taylor and Jefferson streets has elegant rooms decorated with Victorian furnishings.

Other examples of Port Townsend's Victorian past can be seen at the Jefferson County Historical Museum, at Madison and Water streets. This museum displays Victorian furnishings, Indian artifacts, and thousands of old photographs.

Port Townsend's location on the peninsula protecting the Puget Sound made it attractive to the military. Three forts were built to protect the waterway. Now that their service careers are over, the forts are state parks. The best of the three is Fort Worden State Park, on the tip of the peninsula next to town, a park and art center with artists in residence. The Commanding Officer's House has been restored and is open to the public. The fort also has a marine science center and a military museum. The Fort is also the site of the popular Centrum Summer Arts Festival of music, dance, jazz, and theater—it's the longest festival in Port Townsend, held from June to September.

Two other major festivals are the Wooden Boat Festival on the first weekend in September and the Rhododendron Festival in May, which is a wonderful time to visit this small peninsula.

# The Islands of Puget Sound

Picture a getaway on an isolated island, far from busy city streets, surrounded by a vast sound with whales, porpoises, and sea birds of all kinds. In the distance, the snowcovered Olympic and Cascade mountains stand guard at the horizon. Around you the sea traffic is ceaseless—fishing boats, ferries, cruise ships, and naval vessels pass by.

The huge Puget Sound houses more than 200 islands. Most of them are uninhabited, thickly forested, and very isolated. Many are residential or too rustic for a romantic getaway, but a few are outstanding destinations for that special getaway. These special places are Whidbey Island, at 50 miles long the largest island off the U.S. coast, and two of the San Juan Islands, Orcas and San Juan. Here you will find excellent inns and resorts, good restaurants, sensational views of the marine life, and a sense of isolation and serenity that is hard to find on the mainland.

All these islands are linked by ferries (see Ferry Box), and Whidbey can be reached by road via Fidalgo Island on its northern end. Here is a quick summary of the sights of the Islands of the Sound:

**San Juan Island**—The ferry takes you to Friday Harbor, the colorful waterfront village of the busiest and most developed of the islands. The real attraction here is the village itself, a colorful and quaint port town that caters more to tourists than to fishing fleets.

For shoppers, Friday Harbor offers a lot of diversions. The Waterworks Gallery at 315 Argyle Street displays marine art, while the Cabezon Gallery at 60 1st Street West features works by local artists.

The San Juan Historical Museum at 405 Price Street has displays on the early life of island settlers. The Whale Museum at 62 1st Street North is small, but offers interesting and informative displays of whale models, skeletons, and videos. Whales are often spotted off the island from Lime Kiln State Park, the nation's official whale-watching park, six miles outside of town on the west side of the island.

Outside of town, you can explore another little-known aspect of the island's past. The San Juan Island National Historical Park commemorates the little known Pig War between the British and Americans. In the mid-1800s, troops from both nations occupied and claimed the island. In 1859, after an American killed a British soldier's pig, hostilities commenced and lasted for 13 years until Kaiser Wilhelm of Germany acted as mediator and settled the dispute. The hostilities were in name only; no shots were fired. In the park visitors can see the English Camp and the American Camp, both of which are now restored. Historical reenactments and guided hikes are often held at the park. Check with the Chamber of Commerce office at 125 Spring Street for a schedule of activities.

**Orcas Island**—Largest and hilliest of the developed islands, Orcas has numerous campsites, one posh resort (Rosario), more than 30 miles of hiking trails, and a breathtaking view from atop its 2,400-foot-high Mount Constitution. From the old stone lookout tour on the summit you can see the Cascades, the Olympic Peninsula, Vancouver, and Mount Ranier, weather permitting. The log cabins of the Orcas Island Historical Museum in the village of Eastsound display Indian and pioneer artifacts.

(Two other San Juan Islands are also reachable by ferry. Shaw Island is quiet, mostly residential, with visitors staying at the six-spot campground at Indian Cove two miles south of the ferry landing. Franciscan nuns in traditional habits meet the ferry, and run the general store and marina. Lopez Island is a favorite of bicyclists because it is large, flat, and has more than 50 miles of paved roads. Accommodations are in Odlin State Park, a few miles south of the ferry landing, or out Baker View Road, which has developed as well as primitive camp sites.)

**Whidbey Island**—Fifty miles long and a dozen miles wide, this large, mostly agricultural island is known for its fine port towns. Start at the southern end and drive first to Langley, a quiet, attractive town whose bluffside setting makes it a great place for whale watching. Langley's First Street is a mecca for boutiques selling arts and crafts, jewelry, and antiques.

Farther north on Highway 20 is Greenbank, where you will find Meerkerk Rhododendron Gardens, a 53-acre park with hiking trails and ponds. The best time to visit is late April and May, when flowers, bushes, and trees are in the full flush of spring. Next on the road north is Keystone, where the ferry to Port Townsend stops, and then Coupeville, where you will find numerous Victorian homes. The Island County Historical Society Museum at Alexander and Coveland Street has exhibits on the history of Whidbey Island. The Chamber of Commerce at 5 South Main Street has maps outlining walking tours to 27 historic buildings in town. Coupeville is also popular for its nice antique shops and arts and craft stores that line Alexander and Center Streets.

Ebey's Landing National Historical Preserve, just west of Coupeville, contains numerous protected historic buildings and historic sites that are great to wander around.

From here you can drive north to Oak Harbor, the island's largest town, and the adjacent Whidbey Island Naval Air Station. Oak Harbor is big, but lacks charm. You can bypass it and continue across the Deception Pass Bridge to Fidalgo Island and then turn east to the mainland, or continue north to Anacortes and the ferry landing for the San Juan Islands.

## Victoria

A picturesque town that is great for sightseeing or shopping, Victoria is also a town for seeing the trappings of Empire. Located on the southeastern section of Vancouver Island, Victoria is usually visited by travelers who arrive by the ferries from Seattle, Port Angeles, or Vancouver.

As you ride a ferry into Victoria harbor, you'll see the venerable Empress Hotel. Built in 1908 by the Canadian Pacific Railway, this ivy-covered chateau is a powerful symbol of wealth and class from another age.

Another remnant of British rule is the Crystal Garden. When it opened in 1925, the glass-roofed building hosted the largest indoor saltwater pool in the Empire. Today the only things swimming inside this glass palace are the colorful tropical fish in the pools in the tropical gardens. Hundreds of monkeys and scores of birds, including macaws and flamingos, also live among the plants, pools, and waterfalls.

Across Belleville Street is Heritage Court, where you will find the Royal British Columbia Museum and its excellent exhibits on early pioneer and Indian life, prehistoric animals, and artifacts. Next to the museum is Thunderbird Park, a collection of authentic totem poles (Indian carvers sometimes work in the shed on the grounds), and the Carillon, a present to British Columbia from the citizens of Holland. Carillon concerts are played from July through September 16 at 3:00 PM on Sundays, noon on holidays, noon on Wednesdays, and 6:00 PM on Fridays.

At Belleville and Government streets is the Legislative Parliament Building, the seat of government in the province, which is particularly dramatic at night when outlined in hundreds of lights.

Two other attractions in this area are worth visting. Just a few steps away from Parliament on Belleville Street is the Royal London Wax Museum and, behind it on the harbor, the Pacific Undersea Garden, which displays replicas of Victoria, Elvis (he's the King), and other royalty.

But enough sightseeing! Victoria is especially famous for its shopping. Walk north along Government Street at the harbor, where you will find nice woolens at Piccadilly Shoppe British Woolens and George Straight Ltd., Victoriana at Munro's Books, and Inuit art at Gallery of the Arctic. Continue north on Government Street and you come first to the Harbour Square Mall and, a block further, Eaton Centre, which both have scores of fine shops. At View Street, turn left and walk two blocks to Bastion Square, the site of the first Fort Victoria in 1841 and now home to fine boutiques and restaurants.

Art lovers may enjoy visiting the Emily Carr Gallery, which houses works by the noted Impressionists. It's at 1107 Wharf Street on the water.

More fine shops can be found at Market Square (walk two blocks east from Bastion Square and then north two blocks on Government Street). The shops and galleries here are located in carefully preserved nineteenth-century buildings.

A few steps northeast, at Pandora Avenue and Government Street, is Centennial Square, whose buildings date back to the 1880s. The Victoria City Hall, recently restored, was built in 1878. The clock tower was added in 1891.

North of Centennial Square is Fisgard Street, which leads into Victoria's Chinatown. It's a colorful district, full of exotic smells, sights, sounds, and experiences, The narrow Fan Tan Alley that leads off Fisgard was notorious for gambling activities and opium dens long ago.

♣

# FERRYING YOUR WAY AROUND

Ferries are a vital part of the transportation system of the Pacific Northwest. In most cases, you do not need reservations to get aboard except during the summer.

Here is a rundown of the ferries in the Pacific Northwest:

**Washington State Ferries**—Service between Seattle and Winslow on Bainbridge Island and Bremerton; Anacortes to the San Juan Islands and Sidney, B.C. (Vancouver Island); Keystone (Whidbey Island) and Port Townsend; Point Defiance (Tacoma) and Tahlequah; and other ports. Call 202/464–6400 or 800/542–7052 for fares and other schedules.

**Black Ball Transport**—Service between Port Angeles and Victoria on Black Ball Transport. Call 604/386–2202 or 206/622–2222 for fares and schedules.

**Victoria Clipper**—Daily service between Victoria and Seattle on the Victoria Clipper. Call 206/448–5000 or 800/888–2535 for fares and schedules.

**Stena Line**—Daily service between Victoria and Seattle. Call 206/624–6986 or 604/388–7397 for fares and schedules.

**Alaska Marine Highway**—Ferry service throughout southeast Alaska and other points in the state and Canada. Call 907/465–3941 or 800/642–0066 for fares and schedules.

**British Columbia Ferries**—Daily service between Vancouver and Victoria as well as other ports. For fares and schedules, call 604/669–1211 in Vancouver, 604/386–3431 in Victoria, 206/624–6663 in Seattle.

Four other attractions in Victoria will require a car, although bus tours can be arranged through your hotel's tour desk. These attractions are the Art Gallery of Greater Victoria and its fine collection of Japanese and Chinese art and ceramics; the lovely Butchart Gardens, a famous, 50-acre wonderland with more than 5,000 varieties of flowers; the Fable Cottage Estate, which has a 2,000-square-foot thatched home and 3 1/2 acres of beautiful gardens; and the Craigdarroch Castle, a fabulous mansion built in 1890 and recently restored. There are great views of downtown Victoria from its five-story tower.

Outside of town, the wild and rugged 280-mile long Vancouver Island offers some fantastic scenery and a few rustic villages. Within a half-day's drive of the ivy-bedecked Empress are several outstanding inns that are among the best in Canada for accommodations and food. These include the Sooke Harbour House in Sooke, 23 miles west of Victoria, and Hastings House on Salt Spring Island near the artists' colony of Ganges.

Before you leave Victoria, take time to enjoy another remnant of the Empire: high tea at the Empress. It is served precisely at 3:00 PM daily: the scones, jams, and teas are wonderful, and the posh hotel lobby and passing parade of people are a sight to behold.

## For More Information

### On Ashland/Jacksonville:

**Ashland Chamber of Commerce**—110 East Main Street, P.O. Box 606, Ashland, OR 97520. 503/482–3486.

**Jacksonville Chamber of Commerce**—P.O. Box 33, Jacksonville, OR 97530. 503/899–8118.

### On Glacier Bay:

**Glacier Bay National Park**—Gustavus, AK 99826. 907/697–2230.

### On Jasper and Banff National Parks:

**Jasper National Park**—P.O. Box 10, Jasper, AB, Canada T0E 1E0. 403/852–6161.

**Banff National Park**—Box 900, Banff, AB, Canada, T0L 0C0. 403/762–3324.

## On Port Townsend:

**Port Townsend Chamber of Commerce**—Tourism Information Center, 2436 East Sims Way, Port Townsend, WA 98368. 206/385-2722.

## On the Islands of Puget Sound:

**San Juan Islands Tourism Cooperative**—Box 65, Lopez, WA 98261. 206/468-3663.

**North Whidbey Island Chamber of Commerce**—P.O. Box 883, Oak Harbor, WA 98227. 206/675-3535.

**South Whidbey Island Chamber of Commerce**—P.O. Box 403, Langley, WA 98260. 206/321-6765.

## On Victoria, B.C.:

**Tourism Victoria**—612 View Street, Sixth Floor, Victoria, BC V8W 1J5. 604/382-2127.

# Where and When

## In Ashland/Jacksonville:

**Ashland Winery**—2775 East Main Street, Ashland. Open 11:00 AM to 5:00 PM Tuesday through Saturday from April to December; 11:00 AM to 5:00 PM weekends in February and March. Closed in January. 503/488-0088.

**Jacksonville Museum**—206 North 5th Street. Open 10:00 AM to 5:00 PM Tuesday through Sunday. 503/773-6536.

**Oregon Shakespeare Festival**—February through October. Tickets sell out early, so contact the festival at Box 158, Ashland, OR 97520. 800/547-8052.

**Peter Britt Festival**—Late June through Labor Day. Box 1124, Medford, OR 97501. 503/773-6077 or 800/882-7488 (western states only).

**Shakespeare Festival Exhibit Center**—15 South Pioneer Street. Tours 10:00 AM to 4:00 PM Tuesday through Sunday during the festival. 503/482-4331.

**Weisinger's of Ashland**—3150 Siskiyou Boulevard, Ashland. Open 11:00 AM to 6:00 PM Tuesday through Saturday, 12:30 PM to 6:00 PM Sundays from April to September; 11:00 AM to 5:00 PM Friday and Saturday, 12:30 PM to 5:00 PM Sundays from October to March, and by appointment in January and February. 503/488–5989.

## In Glacier Bay National Park:

The park is open year-round, but transportation and facilities are limited except from late May to mid-September.

## In Jasper and Banff National Parks:

**Banff Centre**—St. Julien Road. Call for performance schedule. 403/762–6300.

**Banff Park Museum**—93 Banff Avenue. Open 10:00 AM to 6:00 PM daily. 403/762–3324.

**Columbia Icefields Tours**—Snowcoach and hiking tours offered from May through September. Reserve early. Call 403/762–6700 for the bus tours, 403/762–3056 for the hikes.

**Maligne Canyon Tours**—Daily hikes at 9:00 AM and 1:00 PM December through March. Call 403/852–3370.

**Natural History Museum**—112 Banff Avenue (upper level Clock Tower Mall in Banff). Open daily. 403/762–4747.

**Whyte Museum of the Canadian Rockies**—111 Bear Street. Open 1:00 PM to 5:00 PM Tuesday through Sunday, 1:00 PM to 9:00 PM Thursday. Tours of historic homes offered from 1:30 PM to 4:30 PM Saturday and Sunday. 403/762–2291.

## In Port Townsend:

**Fort Worden State Park**—One mile north of town. Park open daily 6:30 AM to dusk April through Oct. 15, 8:00 AM to 5:00 PM the rest of the year. 206/385–4730. For exhibition and performance schedules, call 206/385–3102.

**Jefferson County Historical Museum**—Madison and Water streets. Open 11:00 AM to 4:00 PM Monday through Saturday, 1:00 PM to 4:00 PM Sunday. 206/385–1003.

**Rothschild House**—Franklin and Taylor Streets. Open 10:00 AM to 5:00 PM daily May through October, 11:00 AM to 4:30 PM weekends the rest of the year. 206/385–2722.

## *In the Islands of Puget Sound:*

**Island County Historical Museum**—908 North West Alexander Street (Alexander and Coveland Streets), Coupeville. Open noon to 4:00 PM daily. 206/678–6854.

**Meerkerk Rhododendron Gardens**—Resort Road, Greenbank. Open daily. 206/321–6682.

**Orcas Island Historical Museum**—Eastsound. Open 1:00 PM to 4:00 PM Monday through Saturday Memorial Day through Labor Day, by appointment the rest of the year. 206/376–4849.

**San Juan Historical Museum**—405 Price Street, Friday Harbor. Open 1:00 PM to 4:00 PM Wednesday through Saturday from June through August. 206/378–3949.

**San Juan Island National Historical Park**—Nine miles northwest of Friday Harbor. Open dawn to dusk daily June through August, weekends in May and September. Call 206/378–2240 for schedule of activities.

**Whale Museum**—62 1st Street North, Friday Harbor. Open daily 10:00 AM to 5:00 PM June through September, 11:00 AM to 4:00 PM daily the rest of the year. 206/378–4710.

## *In Victoria, B.C.:*

**Art Gallery of Greater Victoria**—1040 Moss Street. Open 10:00 AM to 5:00 PM Monday through Wednesday, Friday, and Saturday; 10:00 AM to 9:00 PM Thursday; and 1:00 PM to 5:00 PM Sunday. 604/384–4101.

**Butchart Gardens**—Fourteen miles north on Highway 17. Open daily 9:00 AM to 11:00 PM July and August; 9:00 AM to 9:00 PM June and September; 9:00 AM to 5:00 PM March through May, 9:00 AM to 8:00 PM in December; and 9:00 AM to 4:00 PM the rest of the year. 604/652–4422.

**Craigdarroch Castle**—1050 Joan Crescent Street. Open daily 9:00 AM to 9:00 PM June 15 through Labor Day; 9:00 AM to 7:00 PM the rest of the year. 604/592–5323.

**Crystal Garden—**713 Douglas Street. Open 9:00 AM to 9:00 PM daily June through September 15; 10:00 AM to 5:30 PM the rest of the year. 604/381-1213.

**Fable Cottage Estate—**5187 Cordova Bay Road. Open 9:30 AM to dusk daily mid-March to late October. 604/658-5741.

**Ferry Service—**There is daily ferry service between Victoria and Anacortes on the Washington State Ferry System (206/464-6400 and 800/542-7052); between Victoria and Seattle on the Victoria Clipper (206/448-5000 and 800/888-2535) and on the Stena Line (206/624-6986 and 604/388-7397); between Port Angeles and Victoria on the Black Ball Transport (604/386-2202); and hourly service between Vancouver and Victoria by British Columbia Ferries (604/669-1211 in Vancouver, 604/386-3431 in Victoria).

**Pacific Undersea Gardens—**490 Belleville Street. Open daily 9:00 AM to 9:00 PM June through September, 10:00 AM to 5:00 PM the rest of the year. 604/382-5717.

**Parliament Buildings—**501 Belleville Street. Tours daily. Call 604/387-3046.

**Royal British Columbia Museum—**675 Belleville Street. Open 9:30 AM to 7:00 PM daily May through September; 10:00 AM to 5:30 PM daily the rest of the year. 604/387-3701.

**Royal London Wax Museum—**470 Belleville Street. Open daily 8:30 AM to 10:30 PM July and August; 9:00 AM to 9:00 PM May, June, and September; 9:00 AM to 5:30 PM the rest of the year. 604/388-4461.

## *Romantic Retreats*

Here are our favorite places to stay and dine. But first, an explanation of our cost categories:

One night in a hotel, resort, or inn for two:

*Inexpensive*—Less than $75.
*Moderate*—$75 to $125.
*Expensive*—More than $125.

Dinner for two (wine and drinks not included):

*Inexpensive*—Less than $25.
*Moderate*—$25 to $50.
*Expensive*—More than $50.

## Romantic Lodging in and around Ashland:

**Chanticleer**—This pleasant craftsman-style bungalow offers seven guest rooms, all tastefully decorated with lovely pastel fabrics and French Country pieces. The fireplace is made from river rocks. Moderate. 120 Gresham Street, Ashland, OR 97520. 503/482–1919.

**Jacksonville Inn**—Eight lovingly furnished rooms stuffed with nineteenth-century four-poster beds, antique pieces, and quilts make this an exceptional inn. Moderate. 175 East California Street, Jacksonville OR, 97530. 503/899–1900.

**Livingston Mansion**—Overlooking the Rogue River Valley, this magnificent inn offers three spacious rooms furnished with European pieces. The Regal Suite has a fireplace. There is a nice swimming pool outside. Moderate. 4132 Livingston Road, P.O. Box 1476, Jacksonville, OR 97530. 503/899–7107.

**McCully House Inn**—One of the original six buildings in Jacksonville, this two-story white frame inn was built by a physician whose wife turned it into an inn after he abandoned her (and his bad debts). The decor is wonderfully Victorian with a splash of contemporary. Moderate. 240 East California Street, Jacksonville, OR 97530. 503/899–1942.

**Morical House**—This century-old farmhouse offers five guest rooms, all furnished with antiques, quilts, and other family heirlooms. Lawn games and a small putting green offer diversions on the beautifully landscaped grounds. Moderate. 668 North Main Street, Ashland, OR 97520. 503/482–2254.

**Mt. Ashland Inn**—This huge two-story log cabin offers five guest rooms (all named after nearby mountains), antique quilt-covered beds, and breathtaking views. Guests seeking real privacy may want the guest house, about 400 yards away, with a hot tub on the deck. Moderate. 550 Mt. Ashland Road, Ashland, OR 97520. 503/482–8707.

**Romeo Inn**—There are four rooms and one suite in this charming Cape Cod–style inn. The decor is a mix of contemporary and antique pieces. The nicely shaded lawns have a pool, jacuzzi, and hammock. Moderate (suite is expensive). 295 Idaho Street, Ashland, OR 97520. 503/488–0884.

**Under the Greenwood Tree**—This inn (named after a line in Shakespeare's "As You Like It") is in Medford, about equidistant between Jacksonville and Ashland. Location, though, is the least of its attractions. The inn has four guest rooms in a mainhouse surrounded by ten acres. The barn is from the nineteenth-century. This is a farm, but it is very luxurious. The breakfasts are sensational, for innkeeper Renate Ellam is a Cordon Bleu chef. Expensive. 3045 Bellinger Lane, Medford, OR 97501. 503/776–0000.

**Winchester Country Inn**—Seven antique-furnished guest rooms make this elegant Queen Anne home a special place. Guests can relax in the garden, on the patio, or in the restaurant lounge. Moderate. 35 South Second Street, Ashland, OR 97520. 503/488–1113.

## For Fine Dining in the Area:

**Bayou Grill**—Cajun cooking (although a bit too mild on the spices for our liking), featuring blackened redfish, jambalaya and barbecued frog legs. Close to the Angus Bowmer Theatre. Moderate. 139 East Main Street, Ashland. 503/488–0235.

**Chateaulin**—This intimate cafe down the walkway from the Angus Bowmer Theatre in Ashland is superb. Our favorites are the veal and seafood entrees. The decor is a tasteful wood-and-brick, with copper kettles and ivy serving as trim. Moderate. 50 East Main Street, Ashland. 503/482–2264.

**Green Springs Inn**—Classic Italian cuisine served in the evergreen-covered hills above Ashland. It's a 30-minute drive from town, but the soups and 12 different pastas are worth the trip, particularly for lunch. Moderate. 11470 Highway 66, Ashland. 503/482–0614.

**Jacksonville Inn**—Excellent continental cuisine served in an elegant dining room. Our favorites are the veal picotta and the shrimp in basil sauce. Moderate. 175 East California Street, Jacksonville. 503/899–1900.

**Winchester Country Inn**—This Queen Anne–style inn offers a far-ranging menu, featuring such items as Vietnamese and Chinese dishes as well as more traditional continental items such as roast duck. Moderate. 35 South Second Street, Ashland. 503/488–1113.

## Romantic Lodging in or near Glacier Bay National Park:

**Glacier Bay Country Inn**—This nine-room inn offers pleasant, homey yet modern accommodations in a spacious log cabin. The innkeepers also operate charter boat trips to the glaciers on their elegant yacht and can arrange flightseeing and other tours. Expensive. Box 5, Gustavus, AK 99826. 907/697–2288.

**Glacier Bay Lodge**—This huge log lodge, the only lodge in the park, is surrounded by a thick rain forest. The 55 rooms are comfortable and modern. The boats that head up to the glaciers leave from the docks outside. Expensive. Box 108, Gustavus, AK 99826 or 523 Pine Street, Seattle, WA 98101. 907/697–2225, 800/622–2042.

**Gustavus Inn**—The 13 pleasant rooms at this rural inn are located in the original homestead cabin and the newer lodge. Expensive, but all meals and some activities are included. Box 60, Gustavus, AK 99826. 907/697–2254.

**Puffin's Bed & Breakfast**—There are four rustic but attractive cabins in this quiet retreat in the center of Gustavus. Baths and showers are in separate buildings. Bikes available. Inexpensive. Box 3, Gustavus, AK 99826. 907/697–2260 in the summer, 907/789–9787 in the winter.

## For Fine Dining in the Area:

**Glacier Bay Country Inn**—Very creative cuisine, featuring fresh halibut, salmon, and pasta. Reservations are required if you are not a guest of the inn. Moderate. On the main road between Bartlett's Cove and the airport. 907/697–2288.

**Gustavus Inn**—Family-style meals that are loaded with fresh seafood and vegetables. Reservations required if you are not an inn guest. Moderate. On the main road. 907/697–2254.

## *Romantic Lodging in Jasper National Park:*

**Becker's Roaring River Chalets**—Stay in a rustic cabin or a modern log chalet at this 64-room hotel. Ask for a room with a fireplace. Moderate/expensive. P.O. Box 579, Jasper, AB T0E 1E0. 403/852–3779.

**Jasper Park Lodge**—Some of the views of Lac Beauvert and the Rockies from the rooms here are simply spectacular. The lodge has 416 modern and comfortable rooms, a heated pool, tennis courts, riding stables, golf course, exercise equipment, lawn games, nightclub, and other diversions. Expensive. Box 40, Jasper, AB T0E 1E0. 403/852–3301, 800/828–7447 (from the United States), 800/642–3817 (within Alberta), 800/268–9411 (rest of Canada).

## *For Fine Dining in Jasper:*

**L'Auberge**—Nouvelle continental cuisine, which is excellent even if a bit out of place in a renovated log cabin. Expensive. Three miles south of Jasper on Highway 93. 403/852–3535.

**Le Beauvallon**—Fine continental cuisine, emphasizing beef and seafood. A pianist plays during dinner. Moderate. 96 Geikie Street, in the Chateau Jasper. 403/852–5644.

## *Romantic Lodging in Banff National Park:*

**Banff Springs Hotel**—Picture a century-old Scottish castle perched in the mountains next to a lake and you have the wonderful Banff Springs Hotel. Antiques fill the 834-room hotel, which also has lots of activities: golf, tennis, skiing, game room, exercise equipment, and more. This is a very special place, with an ambience that few modern luxury hotels can match. Expensive. Box 960, AB T0L 0C0. 403/762–2211, 800/828–7447 (from the United States).

**Buffalo Mountain Lodge**—This modern resort overlooks Banff and offers lodging in 85 hillside townhouses. Accommodations range from a single room to two bedrooms with a kitchen. The resort has a hot tub, sauna, and exercise room. Expensive. P.O. Box 1326, Banff, AB T0L 0C0. 403/762–2400, 800/661–1367.

**Chateau Lake Louise**—This huge hotel is on the lake, flanked by rolling lawns and beautiful flower gardens. There are 515 rooms, all nicely furnished. Expensive. Lake Louise, AB T0L 1E0. 403/522–3511, 800/268–9411.

**Emerald Lake Resort**—Located on Highway 1 just west of the Icefields Parkway, this majestic lakeside stone-and-timber chalet was built in 1902 by the Canadian Pacific Railway. Renovated in the early 1980s, and expanded by the addition of 24 chalets, this resort is now first-rate. There are 85 rooms total, all comfortable and all set in a magical location. The resort has a hot tub and exercise room. Expensive. P.O. Box 10, Field, BC, V0A 1G0. 604/343–6321, 800/663–6336.

## *For Fine Dining in Banff and Lake Louise:*

**Banff Springs Hotel**—The four dining rooms here are superb, though expensive. The Alberta Room features continental dishes, the Alhambra specializes in Spanish and continental cuisine, the Rob Roy features beef and flambéed desserts, and the Samurai room has a Japanese menu. All are expensive and in the Banff Springs Hotel. 403/762–2712.

**Le Beaujolais**—Excellent French cuisine in a restaurant known for its magnificent views as well as the movie and stage stars, personalities, and notables who dine there. Expensive. 212 Buffalo Street, Banff. 403/762–2712.

**Post Hotel**—Good French and continental dishes, with an emphasis on Alberta beef and lamb. Entertainment nightly during the peak season. Moderate. 200 Pipestone Road, in the Post Hotel, Lake Louise. 403/522–3989.

**Ticino Swiss-Italian**—This European-style cafe has sensational fondues and veal dishes. Moderate. 205 Wolf Street, Banff. 403/762–3848.

**Victoria Dining Room**—Excellent continental dishes in the main dining room at the Chateau Lake Louise. The prime rib and salmon are wonderful. Entertainment in the evenings, patio dining until 5:00 PM. Expensive. 403/522–3511.

## *Romantic Lodging in Port Townsend:*

**The James House**—This magnificent Victorian has 12 antique-filled rooms, with great water views from the front rooms. Moderate. 1238 Washington Street, Port Townsend, WA 98368. 206/385–1238.

**F.W. Hastings House Old Consulate Inn**—A long title for one of the most celebrated (and photographed) homes in Port Townsend. The eight guest rooms were recently remodeled. The third-floor suite has magnificent views of the water and is a very romantic retreat. Moderate. 313 Walker Street, Port Townsend, WA 98368. 206/385–6753.

**Heritage House**—Six guest rooms, decorated with nice antiques, and offering excellent views of the water and town make this a special place. Moderate. 305 Pierce Street, Port Townsend, WA 98368. 206/385–6800.

**Lizzie's**—There are eight nicely decorated rooms in this stunning Italianate Victorian home built almost a century ago. Moderate. 731 Pierce Street, Port Townsend, WA 98368. 206/385–4168.

**Manresa Castle**—This 42-room hotel was built in 1892 and has recently changed owners. The new innkeepers have reestablished the Manresa as one of the finest inns in the Pacific Northwest. The hotel is located on a hill overlooking the city. The rooms are filled with Victorian pieces and the decor is very romantic. Moderate. P.O. Box 564, Port Townsend, WA 98368. 206/385–5750, 800/732–1281 (in Washington state).

## For Fine Dining in Port Townsend:

**Fountain Cafe**—This cozy restaurant offers sensational fresh seafood (particularly oysters) and some surprisingly spicy dishes. Expect a wait, but it's worth it. Moderate. 920 Washington Street. 206/385–1364.

**Landfall**—Funky local spot serves sensational seafood dishes and a few Mexican entrees, too. Moderate. 412 Water Street. 206/385–5814.

**Manresa Castle**—Continental cuisine served on Friday and Saturday evenings in a beautiful Victorian dining room. Moderate. Seventh and Sheridan streets. 206/385–5750.

**Shanghai Restaurant**—Almost 100 Szechwan and Hunan dishes are on the menu at this popular Chinese restaurant. The decor, though, is more early roadhouse than old forbidden city. Inexpensive. At Point Hudson on the north end of town. 206/ 385–4810.

## Romantic Lodging on the Islands of the Puget Sound:

**Cliff House**—Picture a luxury, three-story house with one wall of glass overlooking the Admiralty Inlet and you have Cliff House. This is a stunning retreat with fantastic views—when there is no fog. It's great for a couple (or two) and has a fireplace, creative decor, and some very deserted beaches. Expensive. 5440 Windmill Road, Freeland, Whidbey Island, WA 98249. 206/321–1556.

**Deer Harbor Lodge and Inn**—The oldest resort on Orcas Island has eight comfortable rooms in a two-story log cabin. One nice touch is the delivery of your breakfast to your doorstep in a picnic basket. Moderate. P.O. Box 142, Deer Harbor, WA 98243. 206/376–4110.

**Duffy House**—This isolated Tudor-style inn above Griffin Bay on San Juan Island has a secluded beach, breathtaking views of the sound and mountains, gardens, and forests. The attractive farmhouse can sleep five couples while the small cabin near the shore sleeps four. Moderate. 760 Pear Point Road, Friday Harbor, WA 98250. 206/378-5604.

**Home by the Sea**—This inn, the first on Whidbey Island, is on the beach at the quaintly named Useless Bay. There are two pleasant guest rooms in the main house, but the real finds here are the inn's four charming cottages located nearby. The Swiss Chalet and the Chantrelle cottages are located in the forest and are wonderful getaways. The Nordic and Cape Cod cottages overlook lakes. Expensive. 2388 East Sunlight Beach Road, Clinton, WA 98236. 206/221-2964.

**Inn at Langley**—This cedar-shingled hotel offers 24 guest rooms, all decorated with Asian furniture. It's all very tranquil. Moderate. 400 1st Street, Langley, Whidbey Island, WA 98260. 206/221-3033.

**Lonesome Cove Resort**—Six lovely cabins make this resort a delightful place. The cabins are next to the water, offering some spectacular views and sunsets. Deer frequent the grounds. Moderate. 5810 Lonesome Cove Road, Friday Harbor, WA 98250. 206/378-4477.

**Olympic Lights**—There are four elegant guest rooms in this isolated Victorian farmhouse furnished with antiques. Only the downstairs room has a private bath. The rooms on the south side of the house have striking views of the Olympic Peninsula and the Strait of San Juan de Fuca. Moderate. 4531-A Cattle Point Road, Friday Harbor, San Juan Island, WA 98250. 206/378-3186.

**Roche Harbor Resort**—This marriage of the 105-year-old Hotel de Haro with cottages and condos offers something for everyone. There are 60 rooms. The renovated hotel rooms have the best views, while the cottages and condos are much nicer. Expensive. P.O. Box 4001, Roche Harbor, San Juan Island, WA 98250. 206/378-2155.

**Rosario Spa & Resort**—This historic Mediterranean-style hotel offers 179 comfortable rooms (though none in the original building), two pools, a spa, whirlpool, sauna, lawn games, tennis and a marina. The rooms are not elegant, but the total resort experience is wonderful. Expensive. Horseshoe Highway, East-sound, Orcas Island, WA 98245. 206/376–2222.

**Saratoga Inn**—The charming shingle-clad inn sits on 25 lovely acres that offer grand views of the Saratoga Passage and the Cascades. The five guest rooms are furnished with antique and country pieces and are cozy. Moderate. 4850 South Coles Road, Langley, Whidbey Island, WA 98260. 206/221–7526.

**Turtleback Farm Inn**—This renovated 100-year-old farm-house offers seven beautiful guest rooms, each different in decor. One has a Northwest theme, another a French touch and a third looks like the cabin of a ship captain. Moderate. Route 1, P.O. Box 650, Eastsound, WA 98245. 206/376–4914.

## For Fine Dining on the Islands:

**Bilbo's Festivo**—This Mexican/New Mexican restaurant was a bit of a surprise (in menu as well as decor). Excellent cooking. Inexpensive. Northbeach Road and A Street, Eastsound, Orcas Island. 206/376–4728.

**Cafe Langley**—Middle Eastern cuisine seems out of place on Whidbey Island, but the quality of the fare will overcome any reluctance you might have. The best dishes are the lamb (particularly the kabobs) and the soups. Moderate. 113 1st Street, Langley, Whidbey Island. 206/221–3090.

**Christina's**—Nouvelle Northwest cuisine, emphasizing fresh seafood, pasta, and excellent desserts. Moderate. Main Street, Eastsound, Orcas Island. 206/376–4904.

**Deer Harbor Lodge and Inn**—The best fresh seafood dishes on Orcas Island are served here. Moderate. Deer Harbor. 206/376–4110.

**Duck Soup Inn**—The specialties are fresh local seafood and poultry at this pretty pondside restaurant outside Friday Harbor on San Juan Island. Expensive. 3090 Roche Harbor Road, Friday Harbor. 206/378–4878.

**Springtree Eating Establishment**—Candlelight and wild-flowers, an ever-changing menu filled with creative dishes, and a cozy Victorian decor make this a very romantic place. Moderate. Under the elm on Spring Street, Friday Harbor, San Juan Island. 206/378-4848.

**Star Bistro**—Good but typical yuppie tavern fare (burgers, salads, and pastas with seafood). Moderate. 201 1/2 1st Street, Langley, Whidbey Island. 206/221-2627.

## Romantic Lodging in Victoria:

**Abigail's**—This wonderful 16-room Tudor hotel offers crystal chandeliers, antiques, and goosedown comforters. Some rooms have canopy beds. We think the third-floor Foxglove Room, with a canopy bed, is the most romantic room. Expensive. 906 McClure Street, Victoria, BC V8V 3E7. 604/388-5363.

**The Beaconsfield**—All 12 rooms in this magnificent Edwardian building are filled with antiques. It's a perfect place for a tryst. Expensive. 998 Humboldt Street, Victoria, BC V8V 2Z8. 604/384-4044.

**The Bedford**—This showplace offers 40 elegant rooms, liveried doormen, flowers, antiques, jacuzzis, and a European flair. Expensive. 1140 Government Street, Victoria, BC V8W 1Y2. 604/384-6835, 800/661-9255.

**Dashwood Manor**—A wonderful Tudor mansion on the water next to Beacon Hill Park, with three guest rooms, each with a fireplace, a great view of the water and mountains, and a very British touch of class. Very quiet and very romantic. Expensive. 1 Cook Road, Victoria, BC V8V 3W6. 604/385-5517.

**Empress Hotel**—Lovely on the outside and a bit time-worn on the inside, this stately grand hotel recently underwent a much-needed facelift. All 488 rooms were renovated and modernized. The Empress is the center of everything in Victoria—politics, tourism, high society parties—and it can often become noisy and crowded. Still, there is nothing like it. Expensive. 721 Government Street, Victoria, BC V8W 1W5. 604/384-8111, 800/268-9411.

**Holland House Inn**—This modernistic inn has ten beautiful rooms, all decorated with avant-garde works of art. Ask for a room with a balcony if you want to replay the Romeo and Juliet scene. Expensive. 595 Michigan Street, Victoria, BC V8V 1S7. 604/384–6644.

**Laurel Point Inn**—There are 202 nicely furnished rooms in this modern hotel next to the harbor. Great views. Expensive. 680 Montreal Street, Victoria, BC V8V 1Z8. 604/386–8721, 800/ 663–7667.

**Oak Bay Beach Hotel**—Great views of the Haro Strait and sunsets, 51 antique-furnished rooms, and a very British atmosphere make this a special place. Expensive. 1175 Beach Drive, Victoria, BC V8S 2N2. 604/598–4556.

## Romantic Lodging Elsewhere on Vancouver Island:

**Hastings House**—This magnificent English-style resort offers ten spacious suites, located in six attractive buildings on Salt Spring Island, about 35 miles north of Victoria. The accommodations are superb, with large sitting rooms, fireplaces, additional baths, and other amenities. Guests can ride bicycles, play croquet, go fishing, canoeing, or golfing, all within a few minutes walk of their suite. Also within a short walk is the village of Ganges, whose artists are well known for the high quality of their pottery, weavings, and carvings. Meals—excellent French dishes with a hint of Northwest cuisine—are served in the elegant Manor House. Expensive. P.O. Box 1110, Ganges, BC V0S 1E0. 604/ 537–2362, 800/661–9255 from United States and Western Canada.

**Sooke Harbour House**—This elegant inn has it all: grand views of the Strait of Juan de Fuca and the Olympic Mountains, cuisine famous far beyond the region, and accommodations in three spacious suites and ten attractive rooms in a new addition. The food, rooms, grounds, and the view are among the best offered in Canada. The suites in the renovated 1931 farmhouse are filled with antiques. The ten new rooms are decorated with fine Indian art. Our favorite room is the Victor Newman Farmhouse, which has a whirlpool bath for two facing a see-through fireplace. Through the flames you can see the bay and mountains.

Expensive, but worth every penny. Breakfast and lunch included. 1528 Whiffen Spit Road, Rural Route 4, Sooke, BC V0S 1N0. 604/642–3421.

## For Fine Dining in Victoria:

**Cafe Laurel**—Located in the Laurel Point Inn, this waterfront restaurant serves the best Sunday brunch in town. Moderate. 680 Montreal Street. 604/386–8721.

**Chez Daniel**—Excellent French cuisine—a rarity in Victoria—in a stylish dining room. Expensive. 2522 Estavan Avenue. 604/592–7424.

**Grape Escape**—Pacific Northwest cuisine served with some Indian and Asian entrees. Moderate. 506 Fort Street. 604/386–8446.

**Herald Street Caffe**—The specials are really exceptional at this Italian and continental dining room. Moderate. 546 Herald Street. 604/381–1441.

**Larousse**—Eclectic menu, with traditional continental dishes and African, Indian, and Asian offerings. Moderate. 1619 Store Street. 604/386–3454.

**La Ville d'Is**—This cozy restaurant serves excellent seafood with a French touch. When the weather is nice, dine out on the cafe tables. Moderate. 26 Bastion Square. 604/388–9414.

**La Petite Colombe**—Simply French and simply wonderful, with lunches better than dinners. Moderate. 604 Broughton. 604/383–3234.

**Metropolitan Diner**—Don't worry about mashed potatoes, gravy, or blue plate specials here. This diner is a trendy spot offering excellent and creative salads, turkey burgers, seafood, and other chic cuisine. It's a good spot for lunch. Moderate. 1715 Government Street. 604/381–1512.

**Pagliacci's**—Ignore the New York Jewish deli-style menu puns (Last Chicken in Paris) and the photos of Hollywood stars on the wall and go for the excellent Italian dishes. Moderate. 1011 Broad Street. 604/386–1662.

**Six Mile Pub**—This 1885 Victorian carriage house offers very good seafood dishes as well as lighter fare. Inexpensive. 494 Island Highway. 604/478–3121.

**Wah Lai Yuen**—Outstanding Cantonese cuisine and huge servings in this spot that's in what is left of Victoria's Chinatown. Inexpensive. 560 Fisgard Street. 604/381–5355.

The vineyard at Chateau Ste. Michelle in Grandview, Washington.
*(Photo courtesy Chateau Ste. Michelle)*

CHAPTER 2

# *Wine Country*

🌲 🌲 🌲 🌲 🌲 🌲 🌲 🌲

*T*he language of love and wine are as intertwined as the vines that grace a winemaker's vineyard. Love, like a vineyard, blossoms, matures, and, with nurturing and personal attention, slowly ripens. With that flush of ripeness comes the realization that love as well as wine can be intoxicating.

As you may have guessed, one of our favorite romantic getaways is to tour the vineyards and wineries of a region. Tasting the new wines isn't the only attraction, of course, for there is only so much of that you can do. The reason to make this trip is that the countryside is lovely, the wineries are interesting, and, with luck, you just might stumble into a festival, for wineries are popular locations for music festivals, arts exhibits, food festivals, and other activities.

Outnumbered but not overshadowed by the famous wineries of neighboring California, the vineyards of Washington and Oregon are attracting national attention. Washington's wine industry now ranks second in the nation in production, and Oregon's viticultural operations are flourishing, not only in bottles produced but in awards won.

The wineries in this region produce fine varietals like chardonnays, pinot noir, and sauvignon blanc. Some cellars are producing sparkling wines by the *method champenoise* process. (Strictly speaking, champagnes come only from that viticultural region of France, though the method to make champagne is used around the world, and the term champagne, whether the French like it or not, is used to describe many white bubbling wines.)

The winery tours we outline in this chapter are in the Yakima Valley of Washington and the Willamette Valley of Oregon, where near-perfect soil, sun, and water conditions have attracted scores of winemakers. This clustering of wineries makes it easier for visitors, who can combine a lovely scenic country drive with a tasting tour of the vineyards.

The wineries we discuss here were not chosen solely for the quality of their wines, for selecting a fine wine is a very personal decision. Rather, these wineries are a sampling—a tasting, if you will—of what the wine country of Washington and Oregon has to offer.

## Washington's Yakima Valley

The fertile Yakima Valley, about one hundred miles southeast of Seattle, is a perfect home for the vine. Here vintners found the rare balance of warm days, cool nights, plentiful water, and cooling breezes that grape vines need to thrive.

These near-perfect conditions have attracted more than 20 wineries that produce and sell wines sold under the Yakima Valley appellation. The wines produced include chenin blanc, pinot noir, merlot, cabernet sauvignon, semillon, and chardonnay.

Before starting a tour, get a brochure on the wineries from the Yakima Valley Wine Growers Association (P.O. Box 39, Grandview, WA 98930) or pick it up at one of the wineries along the way. The wineries are along I-82 in the valley, but are often on sideroads not shown on state maps. The association's brochure has small, detailed maps that will guide you to each stop along the way.

The best time to visit is really up to you and your desires. Most wineries are open at least some time during the week year-round. Spring is a popular time, for the grape leaves are just beginning to come out, casting a light-green haze on the hillside vineyards. Summer is when the vines and the maturing grapes become lush, and late summer and early fall are the harvest months, a popular time for festivals and the busiest for the wine-makers.

The two major wine festivals in the Yakima Valley are the Spring Barrel Testing in late April and the Thanksgiving in the Wine Country festivities in November. All the wineries in the Yakima Valley take part in these festivals.

A tour of the region should start in Yakima, which is attractive enough for a stopover during this tour. Yakima is known for its Front Street Historical District of restored buildings and shops, many of which are in 22 train cars. For a one-stop overview of the area's wineries, drop by The Wine Cellar, at 5 North Front Street. Owner Lenore Lambert holds tastings and dispenses advice on touring the wine country. If you are visiting during the summer, consider taking the Yakima Interurban Trolley Lines, two antique cars that make 19-mile runs through the countryside around Yakima. The rides are offered on summer evenings and weekends.

After a visit in Yakima, take I-82 south. This interstate is the main corridor through the valley and serves as a fast and efficient connection to the wineries. All of the wineries welcome visitors, though the hours vary. For a complete list of hours, telephone numbers, and addresses, please see page 56.

The first stop is at Exit 40, at the town of Wapato. There you will find Staton Hills Winery, a French country-style winery with great views of the valley and a 16-acre vineyard notable for the unusual trellises that hold up the grapes. The three different trellis systems give the grape leaves greater exposure to the sun, and thus produce faster and lusher growth.

Staton Hills produces Johannisberg riesling, chardonnay, merlot, cabernet sauvignon, and other varietals. This cedar-and-stone winery celebrates its anniversary with festivities on the last weekend in June.

Back on I-82, continue south to Exits 50 and 52 and seven of the valley's finer wineries. Six of these wineries are in the town of Zillah. The first is the Covey Run Winery, a large operation that produces a number of varietals and offers tours that allow you to see the wine-making process through windows. The huge deck next to the winery is a great place for a picnic. This winery celebrates Bacchus Day in September.

Elsewhere in Zillah are:

♣ **Zillah Oakes Winery**, whose grapes are grown on Rattlesnake Mountain, has won awards for its fine grenache. This winery is just off Exit 52. Zillah Oakes celebrates its birthday with a party in early May.

♠ **Hyatt Vineyards Winery**, which produces chardonnay, merlot, cabernet sauvignon, and rieslings from its 75 acres of grapes. Hyatt celebrates its birthday with a festival at the end of November.

♠ **Bonair Winery**, a small operation that specializes in chardonnay and cabernet sauvignon. Bonair throws itself a birthday party in mid-August.

♠ **Horizon's Edge Winery**, named after the striking view of Mt. Rainier and Mt. Adams from the tasting room. This winery produces champagne, chardonnays, pinot noir, and other wines. The grape arbor is a popular place for picnicking. Horizon's Edge celebrates its birthday in early August with champagne tasting.

♠ **Portteus Vineyards**, which has won a number of awards for its excellent portteus cabernet made from its 47 acres of grapes.

♠ **Vin de'L'Ouest Winery**, in Toppenish, south of I-82 at Exit 50, known for its art gallery as well as its fine varietals. The gallery displays more than 400 pieces of Indian and Western art and serves as the wine tasting room. The Yakima Indians flourished in this region, and their history is celebrated at the Yakima Nation Cultural Center on the western side of Toppenish.

Continue south on I-82 to Exit 54 and the town of Granger. Here are found Eaton Hill Winery, a newer vineyard that produces rieslings and semillon, and Stewart Vineyards, located atop Cherry Hill and producer of rieslings, cabernet sauvignon, sauvignon blanc, and other wines.

Farther south along I-82 is Grandview, which marks its viticultural heritage with a grape-stomping festival in early September. Grandview is the location of Chateau Ste. Michelle, the state's oldest winery. The operation dates to the end of Prohibition and the winery is famous for its fine reds. The Grandview winery is one of two that Chateau Ste. Michelle operates in the state.

The next town along I-82 is Prosser, which has four wineries. The Yakima River Winery is acclaimed for its barrel-aged red wines. This winery holds barrel tastings in late April, over the July 4th weekend, and at Thanksgiving.

Pontin Del Roza produces chenin blanc, blush wines, and other varietals. They hold an open house with tastings in late May. The Hinzerling Winery makes dessert wines as well as cabernets and throws a harvest party in early October. Chinook Wines produces chardonnay, semillon and merlot. Its garden is a nice place to picnic.

The final cluster on this Yakima Valley tour is around Benton City. Here you will find Oakwood Cellars, the maker of cabernets, merlots, and other varietals, and sponsor of an annual bicycle race every June; Kiona Vineyards Winery, an operation owned by two families and producer of acclaimed varietals; and Blackwood Canyon, which makes chardonnays, semillon, and harvest wines.

If you have the time, return to I-82 and drive south to the Columbia River valley, about 35 miles away. Just before you reach the river, exit west on Highway 14 and drive to Paterson, Washington, where the state's second-largest winery—Columbia Crest—is found. This winery, second only to Chateau Ste. Michelle in annual production, produces seven fine reds and ten wines, with its merlot among the top-sellers in the nation. The winery holds more than a million gallons of wine. The grounds include an attractive picnicking area, a pond with a fountain, and luxurious wine-tasting facilities.

A final sidetrip in this region takes you to one of the most dramatic river canyons in the state. From Yakima, follow Highway 821 north through the Yakima River Canyon to Ellensburg. The scenery is spectacular, and Ellensburg has enough diversions to make the trip worthwhile. Stop by the Kittitas County Historical Museum at East Third and Pine Streets and pick up a guide to the historic district. The downtown was devastated by fire in 1889 and rebuilt with an interesting mix of Art Deco and Victorian building styles. Works by regional and national artists are on display at the Sarah Spurgeon Gallery in the Fine Arts Complex at Central Washington University and at the Community Art Gallery at 408½ North Pearl Street.

Four miles outside of town on the Kittitas Highway is the Olmstead Place, a log cabin dating back to an 1875 ranch. This western heritage comes alive every May when the National Western Art Show and Auction comes to town and on Labor Day weekend when the biggest rodeo in the state is held.

## The Willamette Valley

Oregon's chief viticultural region is in the Willamette Valley, a region about 125 miles long that lies west of I-5 between Portland and Eugene.

It is in these rolling hills and fertile valleys that the grapes find the magical combination of sunny days, cool nights, and moisture borne from the Pacific by nurturing breezes.

Oregon's wines are delicate and known for their fruitiness. Pinot noir, chardonnay, riesling, cabernet sauvignon and other varietals are produced here, along with delicious fruit wines—blackberry, raspberry, boysenberry and loganberry.

Before starting a tour of the wineries of the Willamette Valley, contact the Oregon Winegrowers' Association (1200 NW Front Avenue, Suite 400, Portland, OR 97920) for their excellent brochure on the vineyards. It offers detailed maps to the wineries of the area.

This tour starts at the Ponzi Vineyards, on Highway 210 about 15 miles southwest of Portland. Now more than two decades old, this winery has been acclaimed for its fine pinot noir, pinot gris, and chardonnay. Winemaker Richard Ponzi was recognized in 1988 as one of the top 15 international winemakers by *The Wine Advocate*.

About 15 miles northwest of Ponzi, near the town of Forest Grove, is the Laurel Ridge Winery. A German winemaking family first planted these slopes in the 1800s. Prohibition killed those dreams, though, until 1966 when the vineyards and winery were revived. Laurel Ridge is known for its fine "methode champenoise" sparkling wines as well as semillon, sylvaner, and riesling.

A bit farther west is Shafer Vineyard Cellars, which produces chardonnay, white riesling, pinot noir, gewürztraminer, and sauvignon blanc. You can sample these vintages in the tasting room overlooking the valley. During July and August, jazz concerts are held at the vineyard every Sunday.

The nearby town of Forest Grove is a popular destination in early March when the town has a Barbershop Ballad Contest and Gay Nineties Festival.

Two-and-a-half miles south of Forest Grove is Montinore Vineyards, a breathtaking 588-acre estate whose tree-lined drive leads to a grand Victorian mansion. The winery produces pinot noir, chenin blanc, white riesling, and other varietals.

Continue south on Highway 47 to Gaston and Elk Cove Vineyards, whose wine-tasting room offers spectacular views of the countryside. Elk Cove's owners Joe and Pat Campbell make riesligs, pinot noir, chardonnay, cabernet sauvignon, and other varietals. Picnic tables are available if you want to stop for a meal.

About 20 miles farther south brings you to Highway 99W, the state's official Wine Highway, which heads west toward McMinnville, a haven for B&Bs and home of the International Pinot Noir Celebration in late June. The festival is a major event, featuring wine tastings, as well as lectures and appearances by famous chefs.

McMinnville is also home to Eyrie Vineyards' winery, whose owners, David and Diana Lette, won the 1979 Olympics of the Wines of the World in Paris with their fine pinot noir. Their chardonnay also has won acclaim.

Next to the Eyrie winery is the Arterberry Winery, whose 1985 pinot noir was rated as the Best of the Best by the *Wine Spectator* newsletter. Arterberry's chardonnay has received similar applause.

Farther south on Highway 99W is Ellendale Winery's tasting room, located 2.5 miles south of Rickreall. Ellendale is known for its sparkling wine called "Crystal Mist," a vintage made from pinot noir and chardonnay in the "methode champenoise." Ellendale also makes white riesling, cabernet franc, and wines from honey, mead, Niagara grapes, and "Wooly Booger"—a blend of cherries and berries.

After sampling a bit of Crystal Mist, continue south on Highway 99W and the exit for Albany, where you will find Springhill Cellars. Springhill's pinot noir has won statewide competitions.

Next along Highway 99W is Tyee Wine Cellars, just south of Corvallis. Tyee (a northwest Indian term for "Chief" or "Best") makes pinot noir, chardonnay and other varietals.

From this point you can continue south to Eugene, a pleasant college town in the heart of the thickly forested Emerald Empire. Eugene is known for fine concerts, opera, and ballet at its Hult Center for the Performing Arts and the Oregon Bach Festival every June. In town, the Fifth Street Market offers a tasty combination of food stores and wine shops, crafts, book vendors, and other boutiques and galleries.

If you decide instead to go north to Portland, consider stopping in Salem, the state capital. The top sight in town is the Reed Opera House at NE Court and Liberty Streets, which now features specialty shops—gifts, crafts, clothing, and art—rather than arias.

The Deepwood Estate, at Mission and 12th Streets SE in the northeast corner of Bush Park, has four acres of gardens and a magnificent 1894 Queen Anne–style mansion famous for its stained glass and interior woodwork. You may also want to visit the Salem Art Association's museum in Bush Park. The museum is located in an elegant Victorian house built in 1878. Behind the house is the art center, with exhibits and sales of works by local artists. Each July Salem hosts a major arts fair, which usually attracts hundreds of artists.

Elsewhere in Salem, the Mission Mill Village at 1313 Mill Street SE is a historic site with a working nineteenth-century textile mill and renovated homes. Salem's visitors' center is next to the mill's entrance.

One of Salem's quaintly named wineries, St. Innocent, produces a sparkling wine, pinot noir, and fine chardonnay, and is on 22nd Street SE.

East of Salem, in the perfectly named town of Sublimity, is the Silver Falls Winery. Located in some very scenic landscape in the foothills of the Cascades, the winery is a great setting for a picnic or a festival. Every year, on the weekend after July 4, Silver Falls sponsors a Summer Bluegrass Festival at the winery, where you can sample Silver Falls' pinot noir while listening to some fine musicians.

Your final stop before returning to Portland should be the small town of Aurora, east of I-5, about equidistant between Salem and Portland. Aurora was founded as a Christian commune in 1856, called Aurora Colony. The commune itself lasted only 17 years, but you can tour five of the sect's original buildings, which have been restored. The colony was an important patron of fine art, culture, and craftsmanship, and this appreciation perhaps is seminal in modern-day Aurora, now the center of antiques in central Oregon. Fine American and European items are for sale in the renovated Victorian buildings lining the main highway in town.

A visit to Aurora will make your trip to wine country complete, with a wonderful sampling of fine wines, superb scenery, art, and antiques. Whether you sample the vintages at one winery or several, remember to take time to savor the wine *and* your relationship.

## For More Information

**Yakima Valley Wine Growers Association**—P.O. Box 39, Grandview, WA 98930. (No telephone.)

**Oregon Winegrowers' Assocation**—1200 NW Front Avenue, Suite 400, Portland, OR 97209. 503/228–8403.

♠

# BREWING UP A THIRST

Wineries aren't the only place to lift a glass and taste the latest in spirits. In Seattle, Rainier Brewery, at 3100 Airport Way S (two miles south of the Kingdome via I-5), offers half-hour tours that conclude with free samples of their popular beers. Tours are offered from 1:00 PM to 6:00 PM daily. Call 202/622–2600.

More beers can be found at Seattle's brew pubs, a tradition in the Pacific Northwest. The Pacific Northwest Brewing Company, at 322 Occidental Avenue in Pioneer Square, offers tours on request from 11:30 AM to 2:00 PM and 4:00 PM to 10:00 PM, Tuesday through Saturday. Call 206/621–7002.

Pale ale, porter, amber, and specialty beers that change monthly are on tap at the Big Time Brewery at 4133 University Way NE. The brewery is also a popular tavern with the students at the nearby University of Washington. Call 206/545–4509.

Two better known Northwest brews are the Ballard Bitter and Red Hook Ale found at Trolleyman, a pleasant tavern at 3400 Phinney Avenue N. Tours are offered on weekdays at

## Where and When

### In Washington:

**Blackwood Canyon**—Sunset Road, Benton City. Open 10:00 AM to 6:00 PM daily. 509/588–6249.

**Bonair Winery**—500 S Bonair Road, Zillah. Open 10:00 AM to 5:00 PM daily. 509/829–6027.

**Chateau Ste. Michelle**—West Fifth Avenue and Avenue B, Grandview. Open 10:00 AM to 5:00 PM daily. 509/882–3928.

**Covey Run**—1500 Vintage Road, Zillah. Open 10:00 AM to 5:00 PM Monday through Saturday; noon to 5:00 PM Sunday. Shorter hours in the winter. 509/829–6235.

3:00 PM, and on weekends at 1:30 PM, 2:30 PM, 3:30 PM, and 4:30 PM. Call 206/548–8000.

Tasting and driving don't mix, so consider taking a ride on the Northwest Brewery & Pub Tours. The four-hour van tour of the top pubs and microbreweries is offered on weekend afternoons and Monday nights. Call 206/547–1186.

In Portland, Oregon, two breweries offer tours. The Bridgeport Brewery at 1313 NW Marshall Street has tours from 2:00 PM to 3:00 PM Saturdays and Sundays. Its pub is open 2:00 PM to 11:00 PM Tuesday through Thursday; 2:00 PM to midnight on Friday; noon to midnight on Saturday; and 1:00 PM to 9:00 PM on Sunday. Call 503/241–7179. The Widmer Brewery at 929 N Russell Street has tours at noon and 1:00 PM on Saturdays. Call 503/281–BIER.

In Vancouver, B.C., the Granville Island Brewery at 1441 Cartwright Street on the island offers tours at 2:00 PM weekdays and at 1:00 PM and 3:00 PM on Sundays. Call 604/688–9927.

In Juneau, Alaska, the Alaskan Brewery Co. at 5429 Shaune Drive conducts tours at 11:00 PM and 4:00 PM on Tuesdays and Thursdays. Call 907/780–5866.

**Eaton Hill Winery**—530 Gurley Road, Granger. Open 10:00 AM to 5:00 PM weekends and some weekdays. 509/854–2508.

**Hinzerling Winery**—1520 Sheridan, Prosser. Open 11:00 AM to 5:00 PM Monday through Saturday; 11:00 AM to 4:00 PM Sunday. Closed Sundays December through February. 509/786–2163.

**Horizon's Edge Winery**—4530 East Zillah Drive, Zillah. Open 10:00 AM to 5:00 PM daily. 509/829–6401.

**Hyatt Vineyards Winery**—2020 Gilbert Road, Zillah. Open 11:00 AM to 5:00 PM daily. 509/829–6333.

**Kiona Vineyards Winery**—Sunset Road, Benton City. Open noon to 5:00 PM daily. 509/588–6716.

**Oakwood Cellars**—De Moss Road, Benton City. Open 6:00 PM to 8:00 PM Wednesday through Friday; noon to 6:00 PM Saturday and Sunday; and noon to 6:00 PM Fridays in the summer. 509/588–5332.

**Pontin del Roza**—Hinzerling and McCreadie roads, Prosser. Open 10:00 AM to 5:00 PM daily. 509/786–4449.

**Portteus Vineyards**—5201 Highland Drive, Zillah. Open 10:30 AM to 5:00 PM Monday through Saturday; noon to 5:00 PM Sunday. Call for winter hours. 509/829–6970.

**Staton Hills**—71 Gangl Road, Wapato. Open 11:00 AM to 5:30 PM Tuesday through Sunday during the summer; noon to 5:00 PM during the rest of the year. 509/877–2112.

**Stewart Vineyards**—1711 Cherry Hill Road, Granger. Open 10:00 AM to 5:00 PM Monday through Saturday; noon to 5:00 PM Sunday. 509/854–1882.

**Vin de'L'Ouest Winery**—101 Toppenish Avenue, Toppenish. Open daily 10:30 AM to 5:00 PM 509/865–5002.

**Yakima River Winery**—North River Road, off Wine Country Road in Prosser. Open 10:00 AM to 5:00 PM daily. 509/786–2805.

**Zillah Oakes Winery**—At Exit 52 and I-82 in Zillah. Open 10:00 AM to 5:00 PM Monday through Saturday; noon to 5:00 PM Sunday. Call for winter hours. 509/829–6990.

## *In Oregon:*

**Arterberry Winery**—905 East 10th Avenue, McMinnville. Open noon to 5:00 PM May through December, closed January through April. 503/244–0695, 503/472–1587.

**Elk Cove Vineyards**—27751 NW Olson Road, Gaston. Open 11:00 AM to 5:00 PM year round. 503/985–7760.

**Ellendale Winery**—Highway 99W at Rickreall Road, Rickreall. Open 10:00 AM to 6:00 PM daily April through October; 10:00 AM to 6:00 PM Monday through Saturday and noon to 5:00 PM on Sundays November through March. 503/623–6835.

**Eyrie Vineyards**—On East 10th Avenue next to the Arterberry Winery in McMinnville. Visitors welcome Thanksgiving weekend and by appointment. 503/472–6315.

**Laurel Ridge Winery**—On David Hill Road, off Highway 8, west of Forest Grove. Open noon to 5:00 PM daily and by appointment February through December. 503/359-5436.

**Montinore Vineyards**—On Dilley Road in Dilley. Open noon to 5:00 PM daily May through October; noon to 5:00 PM weekends November through April. 503/359-5012.

**Ponzi Vineyards**—14665 SW Winery Lane, Beaverton. Open noon to 5:00 PM weekends February through December. 503/628-1227.

**Shafer Vineyards Cellars**—On Highway 8, 4.5 miles west of Forest Grove. Open noon to 5:00 PM daily June through September; noon to 5:00 PM weekends October through May. 503/357-6604.

**Silver Falls Winery**—4972 Cascade Highway SE. Open noon to 5:00 PM daily June through September; noon to 5:00 PM weekends October through December and March through May. January and February by appointment. 503/769-9463.

**Springhill Cellars**—2920 NW Scenic Drive, Albany. Open 1:00 PM to 5:00 PM weekends April through October. 503/928-1009.

**St. Innocent Winery**—2701 22nd Street SE, Salem. Open Memorial Day and Thanksgiving weekends and by appointment. 503/378-1526.

**Tyee Wine Cellars**—26335 Greenberry Road, Corvallis. Open noon to 5:00 PM on weekends from May through October, noon to 5:00 PM Friday through Sunday on Thanksgiving weekend. By appointment November through April. 503/753-8754.

## *Romantic Retreats*

Here are our favorite places to stay and dine. But first, an explanation of our cost categories:

One night in a hotel, resort, or inn for two:

*Inexpensive*—Less than $75.
*Moderate*—$75 to $125.
*Expensive*—More than $125.

Dinner for two (wine and drinks not included):

*Inexpensive*—Less than $25.
*Moderate*—$25 to $50.
*Expensive*—More than $50.

## Romantic Lodging and Fine Dining in Oregon's Willamette Valley:

### Albany: Romantic Lodging

**Lilla's**—There are four guest rooms in this attractive Victorian mansion; the decor is simple yet comfortable. Moderate. 206 Seventh Avenue SW, Albany, OR 97321. 503/928-9437.

### Aurora: Fine Dining

**Chez Moustache**—The decor isn't exciting, but the three-course meals at this Aurora dining spot are often sensational. The menu is limited, so call for the day's selections. Inexpensive. Main Street and Highway 99E. 503/678-1866.

### Corvallis: Romantic Lodging

**Hanson Country Inn**—There are four very comfortable guest rooms in this grand 1928 farmhouse overlooking the valley. Moderate. 795 SW Hanson Street, Corvallis, OR 97333. 503/752-2919.

**Madison Inn**—This huge five-story Tudor overlooks the town park in Corvallis. It has seven antique-filled guest rooms. Moderate. 660 Madison Avenue, Corvallis, OR 97330. 503/757-1274.

### Corvallis: Fine Dining

**The Gables**—American fare—prime ribs, chops and seafood, and excellent at that. Moderate. 1121 NW Ninth Street. 503/752-3364.

### Eugene: Romantic Lodging

**Campus Cottage**—Three cozy and antique-furnished guest rooms make this B&B a special find. Moderate. 1136 East 19th Street, Eugene, OR 97403. 503/342-5346.

**Lorane Valley Bed & Breakfast**—One may find serenity in this private apartment in a large contemporary home on a wooded hillside outside of town with wonderful views of the valley. Moderate. 86621 Lorane Highway, Eugene, OR 97405. 503/686–0241.

**Mapletree Inn**—This extensively renovated Queen Anne Victorian offers six guest rooms, all tastefully decorated with antique oak furniture. Moderate. 412 East 13th Avenue, Eugene, OR 97401. 503/344–8807.

## Eugene: Fine Dining

**Chantrelle**—This beautiful, intimate dining room serves unusual seafood and wild game dishes. Moderate. 207 East Fifth Avenue. 503/484–4065.

**Excelsior Cafe**—Inventive Northwestern cuisine served in an attractive Victorian in the college district. The menu is eclectic and the Sunday brunch is fabulous. Moderate. 754 East 13th Avenue. 503/342–6963.

**Zenon Cafe**—Pick a cuisine and you will find it here: Italian, Cajun, Indian, American, West African, and more. All of the dishes are good, with the pastas the most consistent winners. Moderate. 898 Pearl Street. 503/343–3005.

## McMinnville: Romantic Lodging

**Mattey House Bed & Breakfast**—Sumptuous breakfasts make this recently restored 1890 Victorian a luxurious place. There are four guest rooms, three of which are decorated with antiques. Moderate. 10221 NE Mattey Lane, McMinnville, OR 97128. 503/434–5058.

## McMinnville: Fine Dining

**La Maison Surrette**—A Victorian house filled with antiques complements the marvelous French prix fixe meals at this lovely dining room. Dinner served weekends only. Moderate. 729 East Third Street. 503/472–6666.

**Lavender's Blue, a Tea Room**—This large, rambling house has been converted into an elegant lavender-and-blue, lace-festooned tea room. The cakes, tortes, and scones are wonderful. Inexpensive. On Cowls Street one block east of Highway 99W. 503/472-4594.

**Nick's Italian Cafe**—The casual atmosphere belies the high quality of the five-course, fixed-price classic Italian dinners served here. Try the rich minestrone soup and leave room for the killer desserts. Moderate. 521 East Third Street. 503/434-4471.

## Salem: Romantic Lodging

**State House Bed & Breakfast**—These four spacious guest rooms and two cottages overlook a garden with a gazebo, hot tub, and a creek in the heart of the capital city. The rooms are pleasantly furnished. One of the cottages has two bedrooms while the other has two units with a total of three bedrooms, which can be rented as a unit. Moderate. 2146 State Street, Salem, OR 97301. 503/588-1340.

## Salem: Fine Dining

**Alessandro's Park Plaza**—You don't really order a dinner at this elegant restaurant. Each night three different multicourse meals are prepared. You can choose your entree, but the rest of the meal is a surprise. It's an unusual technique, which guarantees a sensational, creative dinner featuring the best and freshest local food. Moderate. 325 High Street. 503/370-9951.

**Inn at Orchard Heights**—Continental-style cuisine served in a lovely setting next to an orchard. Moderate. 695 Orchard Heights Road NW. 503/378-1780.

**Pilar's**—Excellent pasta and salads are served at this small dining spot. Inexpensive. 189 Liberty Street North. 503/363-7578.

# Romantic Lodging and Fine Dining in Washington's Yakima Valley:

## Granger: Romantic Lodging

**Rinehold Cannery Homestead**—This large farmhouse offers two pleasant guest rooms that share a sitting area with great views of the farm and countryside. Moderate. 530 Gurley Road, Route 1, Box 1117, Granger, WA 98932. 509/854-2508.

## Prosser: Romantic Lodging and Fine Dining

**Wine Country Inn**—This turn-of-the-century home on the Yakima River has four cozy rooms, and also has a popular continental restaurant. Inexpensive. 104 Sixth Street, Prosser, WA 99350. 509/786-2855.

## Yakima: Romantic Lodging

**MeadowBrook Bed & Breakfast**—This large Dutch Colonial home has four guest rooms, each with a view of the garden and orchards. Each room has pleasant decor and views of the garden and hills. Inexpensive. 1010 Meadowbrook Road, Yakima, WA 98903. 509/248-2387.

**Tudor Guest House**—This dignified mansion offers five tasteful guest rooms, all furnished with antiques. Moderate. 3111 Tieton Drive, Yakima, WA 98902. 509/452-8112.

## Yakima: Fine Dining

**Birchfield Manor**—Excellent French country cuisine served in a very elegant antique-filled home. There are four selections daily on the prix fixe menu. Expensive. 2018 Birchfield Road. 509/452-1960.

**Gasperetti's Restaurant**—Fresh pastas, fresh seafood, and sensational daily specials are served in this fine northern Italian dining room. Moderate. 1013 North First Street. 509/248-0628.

**Greystone**—The decor is early 1900s, but the menu features nouvelle cuisine. The daily specials focus on seafood, but the apple-and-sausage-stuffed chicken breast and the pork tenderloin are also excellent. Moderate. 5 North Front Street. 509/248-9801.

The Space Needle towers over Seattle, with the spectacular Mt. Rainier in the distance. *(Seattle-King County News Bureau—James Bell)*

# CHAPTER 3

# *Tales of Four Cities*

*T*here are four gems in the crown of the Pacific Northwest: Edmonton, Portland, Seattle, and Vancouver—cities with incredible scenery, excitement-filled streets, excellent museums, attractive parks, great shops, rediscovered historic neighborhoods, and a lifestyle celebrating the best of urban life and nature.

Though smaller in population than many of the metropolises found in the East or California, all four cities are very sophisticated and offer countless opportunities for outdoor activities and adventures inside or just outside the city limits. All four cities are also home to a vibrant cultural life, with excellent museums, flourishing theater companies, symphony orchestras, operas, and ballet.

These cultural activities, historical neighborhoods, interesting shops, and festive events make these cities well worth a week or weekend visit.

## Edmonton

This 200-year-old town is filled with fine parks, historic neighborhoods, great museums, and a grand indoor garden. Unfortunately, most visitors to Edmonton flock to the most popular attraction in the entire Pacific Northwest—the massive West Edmonton Mall.

The West Edmonton Mall, at 87th Avenue and 170th Street, can best be described in numbers: more than 20 million visitors a year, 800 specialty stores, 11 major department stores, 110 restaurants or dining spots, 34 cinemas, a five-acre Waterpark with a wave pool that surfers use, an ice rink, a lake with 200 forms of marine life in which you can take a submarine ride, an 18-hole miniature golf course, a Fantasyland amusement park with a ferris wheel and the world's tallest indoor roller coaster, a lake with an 80-foot replica of the Santa Maria, a zoo, a dolphin show, hot tubs, and (need we say it) more.

The mall is captivating, and unfortunately overshadows Edmonton's many fine riverfront parks, museums, and historic sites. Edmonton was founded in 1795 as a fur-trading outpost by the Hudson Bay Trading Company. A century later, when the fur trade dwindled, the town boomed again as a major supply stop for those seeking their fortune during the Klondike Gold Rush.

Fort Edmonton Park, at Whitemud Drive and Fox Drive on the south bank of the North Saskatchewan River, helps recreate these early years for visitors. The fort (the sixth fort built by the Hudson Bay Trading Company to bear the name Edmonton House) contains a restored village, a copy of the fort built in 1846, costumed actors and guides, and streets recreated to serve as ministages for a look at life in later eras in the city's history.

The Fort Edmonton Park is but one of a series of parks along the river. (Edmonton claims more parkland per capita than any other city in North America.) The riverfront parks offer an amazing array of attractions. From Fort Edmonton Park, you can walk to see wildlife at the adjacent John Janzen Nature Centre or the Valley Zoo across the river, go horseback riding and hang gliding in Whitemud Park, or take a toboggan ride in winter at Emily Murphy Park.

Other major attractions aren't far away. The Muttgart Conservatory, a series of four glass pyramids at 98 Avenue and 96A Street, is a botanical garden displaying flora of different climates. Across the river is the John Walter Museum, 91 Avenue and Walterdale Road, with exhibits on the Victorian age in Edmonton, and the Edmonton Art Gallery, at 2 Sir Winston Churchill Square, displaying fine and applied arts. Farther away is the Edmonton Space & Science Center, at 142 Street and 112 Avenue. The center has an Imax theater, laser light shows, planetarium, and other exhibits.

The Rutherford House, a 1911 Jacobean revival structure at 11153 Saskatchewan Drive, was the home of A.C. Rutherford, Alberta's first premier. Costumed guides lead tours of this magnificent mansion, which is furnished in the style of Rutherford's time. A bit farther east, at 12845 102 Avenue, is the Provincial Museum of Alberta, which has four galleries with exhibits on the area's heritage and history. The lovely gardens outside are filled with sculptures by Alberta artists.

Edmonton celebrates its history in late July in its Klondike Days, a 10-day festival, which features a carnival, raft and horse races, a parade, and other entertainment.

More of Edmonton's past is celebrated at the Ukrainian Canadian Archives & Museum at 9543 110 Avenue and at the Ukrainian Museum of Canada at 10611 110 Avenue. The first museum has exhibits on the Ukrainian immigrants who helped settle Alberta in the nineteenth century while the second celebrates the art and culture of that distant land. A more extensive look at the Ukrainian heritage is visible at the Ukrainian Cultural Heritage Village, 31 miles east of town on Highway 16. The pre-1930s lifestyle of the immigrants is portrayed in a restored town, farm, and more than 30 reconstructed buildings. Costumed guides lead tours and give demonstrations of life in those times.

Another historic area is called Old Strathcona, between 101 and 106 streets and Saskatchewan Drive and 80 Avenue. Buildings from the late nineteenth century line the streets of this former town that was annexed by Edmonton in 1912. Strathcona Square at 8150 105 Street is anchored by the Old Post Office, a magnificently restored Victorian structure that now houses some interesting shops. The Old Post Office is the centerpiece of shopping in downtown Edmonton. Along 82 Avenue (also called Whyte Avenue) you will find an array of shops and boutiques selling fine art, clothing, books, and gifts as well as some nice cafes and coffee bars.

It is the sum of Edmonton's different parts—fine art, historic neighborhoods, grand parks, and the mall—that makes it a fantastic getaway.

# Portland

The City of Roses has a magnificent setting: the Columbia and Willamette rivers come together here, creating an exceptional deepwater port. Nearby are Mt. Hood and other Cascade peaks. Within the city itself are well-preserved historic neighborhoods, stunning rose and flower gardens, more than two hundred fine parks, and art seemingly everywhere—on the streets, in office buildings, in parks, and in playgrounds. Outside the city, a drive east in the scenic Columbia River Gorge takes you to parks, waterfalls, old cities, and a surprising museum.

Start a visit to this fascinating city by touring the historic neighborhoods next to the Willamette River and the Tom McCall Waterfront Park, a popular area for joggers and bicyclists. One of the most popular attractions in the park is the one hundred jets of the fountain at SW Salmon Street. The shower of water is irresistible to children on warm days.

From the fountain, walk north along the river to SW Front Avenue, where the Yamhill Historic District begins, a small but interesting area featuring tall nineteenth-century, Italianate Victorian buildings made of cast iron. The building material was a fortunate choice, for it enabled these structures to survive major fires in 1872 and 1873. A block west of the river is the Yamhill Marketplace, at 110 SW Yamhill Street. The market is a popular destination for shoppers seeking flowers, wearable art, and made-in-Oregon items.

From Yamhill Marketplace you can walk north along SW Second Avenue, passing some interesting art galleries on your way to the Skidmore Historic District that starts north of Oak Street. One gallery worth a visit on your way to the Skidmore District is the Quintana Gallery of Native American Art at 139 SW Second Avenue.

The Skidmore Old Town Historic District is where the original New England settlers founded Portland in 1845. The 20-square-block riverfront area bounded by Oak and Everett streets has been renovated and is now home to some interesting nineteenth-century buildings. The Oregon Maritime Museum (at Oak Street and the river) is a cast-iron building with exhibits on the ships that sailed the rivers here. The Central Fire Station and Skidmore Fountain at 111 SW Front Street are both interesting, and don't miss the antique fire equipment inside the station. The fountain square is the site of the popular Portland Market, held every Saturday and Sunday from March through December. Hundreds of vendors sell jewelry, collectibles, arts, and junk (some plain, and some *tres chic* junk). More arts and crafts can be found inside the Fountain Square Building at 28 SW First Avenue or at the nearby New Market Theater Village, a once-grand stage now home to shops and dining spots. It's at 50 SW Second Avenue.

There are a variety of diverse and interesting neighborhoods in Portland. A few blocks northwest of the Skidmore Fountain is Chinatown, a small and exotic neighborhood marked by the gate at NW Fourth Avenue and Burnside Street. Five blocks south of the Chinatown Gate is the Glazed Terra Cotta National Historic District between Oak and Yamhill streets and SW Fifth and Sixth avenues. The buildings here are ornate terra cotta structures.

From these old buildings you can walk along SW Fifth and Sixth avenues and enjoy a number of outdoor sculptures. The Metropolitan Center for Public Art, on the second floor of the Portland Building at 1120 SW Fifth Avenue, has exhibits on the city's outdoor art and is the unofficial starting point of any walking tour of these public works. The Pioneer Place at 700 SW Fifth Avenue is an upscale shopping mall, with more than 80 shops.

More art can be found at the Oregon Art Institute, at 1219 SW Park Avenue and Jefferson Street. The institute houses the Portland Art Museum, which has an extensive collection of Indian, African, Asian, and contemporary art. Across the tree-shaded South Park at SW Broadway Avenue and SW Main Street is the Portland Center for the Performing Arts. The center is the home of the Portland Shakespeare Festival and presents plays, lectures, opera, ballet, and concerts on its three stages.

Another nearby museum is the Oregon Historical Society at 1230 SW Park Avenue, with exhibits on Oregon's history. The oldest building in town is the Pioneer Courthouse at Fifth Avenue and Morrison Street. Built in 1873, the courthouse is the centerpiece of the square, at the crossroads of Portland. At noon, a wacky weather machine sounds off and then shows a symbol— a sun, a dragon, or a blue heron—to forecast the weather.

Although it has a fine collection of art, Portland is more famous for its extensive gardens. The International Rose Test Gardens, in Washington Park at 400 SW Kingston Avenue off Burnside Road, is the best known with more than four hundred different types of roses planted on the three terraces in the four-acre gardens which were created in 1917. The views of the city from these gardens are magnificent.

The City of Roses celebrates every June with a three- to four-week-long Rose Festival that includes a parade, an Indy 500-type car race, hot air balloon races, concerts, and grand displays of roses.

Adjacent to the Rose Gardens are the Japanese Gardens, reachable by shuttle bus or foot path only. These five meticulously planted gardens also offer grand views of the city below. Don't miss the ceremonial teahouse.

Also be sure to visit the park's Washington Park Zoo; the Hoyt Arboretum with ten miles of trails, an extensive collection of conifers, and more than 500 species of plants; and the World Forestry Center, which has exhibits on the state's logging history.

Other attractions lie in the park north of Burnside Road. There, on a 1,000-foot-high summit overlooking the city, you will find the Pittock Mansion at 3229 NW Pittock Drive. The French Renaissance-style mansion, furnished with fine seventeenth- and eighteenth-century antiques, was built in 1914 by Henry Pittock, creator of the *Portland Oregonian* newspaper.

More attractions await outside of town. Take I-84 east from Portland to the Columbia River Scenic Highway. This highway, the first paved road in Oregon's Cascade Mountains, offers great views of the river, numerous waterfalls, and seven state park areas with great hiking trails. Multnomah Falls is one of the more dramatic cascades you will pass. It plunges 620 feet in two steps. A trail next to the base of the falls leads up to the footbridge spanning the ravine, with a side trail to a viewing platform. The

Nature Center near the base of the falls has exhibits on the area's geology and the Indians who lived there. A few miles beyond the waterfall is the Oneonta Gorge, where a trail leads a half-mile to another stunning waterfall.

East of the gorge, the Scenic Highway merges with I-84. You can continue east past the Bonneville Dam and the town of Cascade Locks. There you can take a river cruise on the stern-wheeler Columbia Gorge. The ship leaves from the Marine Park in town.

The next landmark on the drive east is the Hood River, where you can stop by Columbia Gorge Sailpark in Port Marina and watch the windsurfers (also called boardsailers) battle wind and river. One of the final attractions in the Columbia River gorge is The Dalles, the town that was the terminus of the Oregon Trail. The Dalles is an attractive town, filled with fine nineteenth-century buildings and homes. You can complete your trip with a visit just across the river. Take Highway 197 just east of The Dalles across the river to Highway 14, turn east, and drive 17 miles to Maryhill. At 35 Maryhill Museum Drive, you will find the Maryhill Museum of Art, a delightful and eclectic collection of Rodin sculptures, Russian icons, some personal possessions of Queen Marie of Romania, European and American paintings, and Native American artifacts.

Another Portland-area attraction that is worth seeing is Vancouver, Washington, just across the Columbia River from downtown Portland. Take I-5 north to Exit 1-C and follow the signs to the Ft. Vancouver Historic Site and Officers' Row Historic District. The fort is a re-creation of the base built in 1825 by the Hudson Bay Trading Company. Park service rangers lead tours of the park.

Officers' Row is a collection of more than 20 Victorian homes built between 1850 and 1906, which were used as military residences by such famous generals as Ulysses S. Grant and George C. Marshall. These fine buildings are now private homes, shops, and restaurants.

## *Seattle*

Water, water everywhere.

Seattle is the city of hills with water views everywhere, the city on the sound, the city by the lake or on the river, and the city that gets a lot of rain. Easterners and Westerners alike joke Seattle's weather. One t-shirt we saw announced the "Seattle Rain Festival: January-December." In fact, Seattle gets only about 36 inches of rain a year, less than New York City or Chicago, and most of the precipitation falls between October and March. The rest of the year, particularly from June through September, Seattle's skies are often clear blue, creating a vista demanding you to stop and look.

The waterscape visually complements this vibrant city. Seattle has a fascinating waterfront, a museum-filled center, a restored historic district whose roots stretch back to the Gold Rush days, and a coffee shop on almost every corner. Colorful banners and flower-filled pots add vibrant touches to this lovely city.

Start your tour of this beautiful, interesting town at the Space Needle, the landmark symbolizing Seattle's emergence as a first-rate city. This 605-foot-high tower was built for the 1962 World's Fair. An observation deck at the 520-foot level offers outstanding views of the city, the Cascade Mountains, and Puget Sound.

The kitschy Space Needle is just one of the buildings in the Seattle Center—a 74-acre museum, exhibit hall, and theater complex built for the 1962 World's Fair. The Pacific Science Center explains and demonstrates scientific principles through interactive displays. The Northwest Craft Center displays creative works by local artists. The Fun Forest Amusement Park offers a wide variety of amusing rides.

The best way to travel between the Seattle Center and downtown is via the Monorail, which was also built for the 1962 fair. It makes the trip to Fourth Avenue and Pine Street in 95 seconds. From that terminal you can walk west to the Pike Place Market, where another fascinating aspect of Seattle culture awaits.

Along the way to Pike Place, at 1320 Second Avenue, is the new Seattle Art Museum. The modern building, which opened in late 1991, has a large collection of Indian, Asian, African, and pre-Columbian art.

The cross-streets on the way to the market also have some interesting shops. First Avenue is lined with antique shops north of the market and nightclubs just south of the market. Post Alley, a narrow two-block-long alley between Virginia and Pine streets, has some interesting shops and restaurants. One must-see is the Made in Washington store at Post Alley and Pine Street, where you can purchase local arts and crafts, Washington wines, alder-smoked salmon, and wild berry jams.

At the foot of Pine Street is the world-famous Pike Place Market, a hurly-burly bazaar featuring everything from live Dungeness crabs and huge salmon, to fresh vegetables and fine crafts. Allow plenty of time to browse through the stalls and sample the sights, tastes, and smells of this exotic area.

Although the market may appear at first a confusing collection of local wares, it is in fact fairly organized. The new South Arcade on First Avenue has upscale boutiques. The Sanitary Market (so named because horses were never allowed inside) is home to vendors selling a variety of collectibles and junk. Pike Place, the brick street bissecting the market, has crafts shops, delis, and Mexican and Indian groceries. The Main Arcade (look for the Market Clock) has fishmongers, produce, and craft stalls. The Economy Market and Atrium at First Avenue and Pike Street houses a variety of stores selling toys, books, herbs, and other items. Art galleries can be found on Western Avenue in the north market area. Also at the north end of the market is the Victor Steinbruck Park, which has totem poles, outdoor sculptures, and great views of the waterfront and Elliott Bay (the arm of Puget Sound Seattle is on).

From the market you can walk down to the waterfront. You can either walk along this waterfront, enjoying the many shops and attractions, or ride the Waterfront Trolleys that run between Pier 70 and Pioneer Square, or even climb aboard a rickshaw pulled by a college student.

Pier 70, the trolleys' northern terminus, is a large shipping terminal that has been converted into a complex of art galleries, shops, and restaurants. Farther south on the waterfront is Pier 59 and the Seattle Aquarium, which features the Northwest's marine life, and next to it the Omnidome Film Experience, where you can explore the marine life of the Sound or relive cinematically the explosive eruption of Mount St. Helens.

Pier 58 is where the historic ship Portland landed on July 17, 1897, bringing news of the Klondike gold strike. At Pier 56 you can catch the boat for the Tillicum Village Tours, a four-hour trip to Blake Island that includes a visit to an Indian village, a seafood dinner, dances, wood carving demonstrations, and other Indian folk culture.

At Pier 55 you can take an interesting Seattle Harbor Tour, a one-hour journey around Elliott Bay and the port. You can also catch the Washington State Ferries to the Olympic Peninsula and islands in the Sound at Pier 52. At Pier 48 you will find the Stena Line, which offers daily roundtrip ferry service for passengers and vehicles to Victoria, B.C. The Victoria Clipper catamaran makes a daily roundtrip passenger service to Victoria from Pier 69.

Many shops and taverns line the waterfront here. Ye Olde Curiosity Shop at Pier 54 is a warren of touristy gewgaws and some truly bizarre displays. It's too tacky to miss. Next door, Alaskan Way offers some fine Indian and Eskimo arts and crafts.

The next attraction along the waterfront is Pioneer Square, a 30-block restored area built after the Great Fire of 1889. The original square is now a small triangle, between First and James street, now home to a Tlingit Indian Totem Pole and a statue of Chief Seathl, whose name inspired Seattle's. The Great Fire of 1889 destroyed many of the buildings in the area. Those that exist today were built atop the original abandoned structures left after the disaster. You can also take the unusual Underground Seattle Tour, which includes a walk through the subterranean ruins, some humorous historical anecdotes, and a lot of stair climbing.

The Klondike Gold Rush National Historic Park, located in a storefront at 117 S Main Street in Pioneer Square, offers exhibits, gold-panning demonstrations, and a film on Seattle's role in the 1897 strike.

The square is a haven for art galleries, clothing and antique shops, upscale restaurants and taverns, nightclubs, and sidewalk cafes. Pioneer Square Park, one of two cobblestone parks in the area, houses a wrought-iron bus shelter, a Tlingit totem pole, and 1909 street lights. Fine shops like Madame & Co. (antique lace and linens) and We Hats can be found around the square. First Avenue is home to many of the city's nightclubs as well as the Northwest Gallery of Fine Woodworking, the Magic Mouse Toy Store, and other interesting shops. Many more shops can be found in the Grand Central Arcade Building at First Avenue and Main Street and the Pioneer Building at 600 First Avenue.

Just west of Pioneer Square is the massive Kingdome, the indoor stadium where Seattle's professional baseball and football teams play. The other attraction in this area of Seattle is the International District, a 40-square-block area populated by Chinese, Filipinos, and other Asian nationalities. Here you will find Uwajimaya, a huge Japanese supermaket at 519 Sixth Avenue S, a good place to pick up fresh sushi for a light meal.

Asian culture can be explored at the Nippon Kan Theater at 628 S Washington Street. This cultural center was built in 1909 and hosts kabuki and other forms of Asian theater. Also stop by the Wing Luke Museum, at 407 Seventh Avenue S, which has exhibits on Asian history and culture.

That's the end of the walking tour of Seattle's waterfront area. For shoppers, the commercial heart of Seattle is centered around Fourth and Fifth avenues and Pine Street, with art galleries, boutiques, and antique shops anchored by the Nordstrom at 1501 Fifth Avenue and the Westlake Center, a 75-shop mall at 400 Pine Street. More upscale shops and boutiques can be found at the City Centre mall at Sixth Avenue and Union Street and at Rainier Square at Fifth Avenue and Union Street.

The shops include some world-famous names: Burberrys of London (409 Pike Street), Bally of Switzerland (in the Four Seasons Olympic Hotel at 411 University Street) and Gucci (City Centre).

Seattle has more attractions, of course, but they require transportation. On the north side of metropolitan Seattle are the Hiram M. Chittenden Locks, which permit boat traffic on the Lake Washington Ship Canal that links the lake with the Puget Sound. The lock operation is fascinating to watch. The locks are bordered on the north by a seven-acre garden, on the south by a promenade leading down to the Fish Ladder, which assists salmon and trout in migrating upstream. Viewing ports allow you to see this amazing ritual of nature.

Seattle's major museums include the fine nineteenth- and twentieth-century paintings and textiles at the Henry Art Gallery, at 15th Avenue NE and NE 41st Street, and the Thomas Burke Memorial Washington State Museum, an anthropological and natural history exhibit hall at 17th Avenue NE and NE 45th Street. Both are on the University of Washington campus north of downtown Seattle. Near the university stadium, at 2700 24th Avenue E, is the Museum of History and Industry, which has exhibits from Seattle's early days. South of downtown (via I-5, watch for the signs) is the Museum of Flight, Boeing's 20-plane collection that includes some of the earliest airplanes.

Seattle also has some fine parks. One of our favorites is the Washington Park Arboretum at 2300 Arboretum Drive E. The scenic drive is open during the daylight hours, taking you through interesting landscaping and gardens and offering occasional glimpses of Lake Washington, the huge body of water that borders Seattle on the east. One serene oasis is the Japanese Garden, with waterfalls, a teahouse, and an azumaya (or resting place). Another popular park stop is Discovery Park, which offers views of Puget Sound and maritime traffic, at West Government Way and 36th Avenue W northwest of downtown Seattle. This 534-acre park includes a two-mile beach, nature trails, a fitness course, woods and meadows, the Coast Guard's West Point Light Station, and the Daybreak Star Indian Cultural Center. Indian arts and crafts, including some stunning creations, can be found at the center's excellent Sacred Circle Indian Art Gallery.

For day trips out of Seattle, you can head over to the Olympic Peninsula or visit the Puget Sound islands via ferries or take a drive. La Conner, about 40 miles north of Seattle via I-5, is a small arts community and fishing village at the mouth of the Skagit River. The shops and restaurants are well worth a visit. On the way back take I-405 to Route 502 and Woodinville for a visit to the Chateau Ste. Michelle Winery, at 1411 NE 145th Street. This elegant French Chateau, built in 1912 by a lumber baron, sits on 87 magnificently landscaped acres. The winery tasting room is open daily from 10:00 AM to 4:30 PM. Across the street is the Columbia Winery. Its tasting room is open from 10:00 AM to 5:00 PM daily.

Another possible daytrip is to Snoqualmie Falls, about 30 miles east of Seattle via I-90 (take Exit 27). The falls are a familiar sight to fans of the television series "Twin Peaks." The falls, one hundred feet higher than Niagara, are used to create electric power. The Salish Lodge at the falls offers fine dining and shopping but be careful to stay only in one of the eight suites of the inn's 91 rooms that overlook the cascade. The other 83 rooms face the electrical transformers immediately upriver, spoiling what would otherwise be an exceptionally romantic view.

## Vancouver

Vancouver may be the most beautiful city on the planet—but only when the sun shines.

Like Seattle, Vancouver gets a lot of rain from fall to early spring. The rest of the year the skies are clear and Vancouver blossoms. This magnificent town is filled with attractions to meet any whim: sidewalk cafes, busy streets lined with grand stores and upscale boutiques, serene wilderness parks, renovated historic neighborhoods, and an exotic Chinatown. Minutes away are more natural wonders: snow-capped mountains even in the summer, rushing rivers with spawning salmon, and the busiest ski resort in North America.

This city has it all. But with so much to see, where do you start? Why not with the street that summarizes the best of this city?

♠

# SEATTLE'S CAFFEINE HABIT

Seattle has a habit. It's not the Space Needle and it's not the Seahawks.

It's coffee.

Seattle has the highest per capita consumption of gourmet coffee beans in the country. This coffee craze began in the 1960s and has spread to the point where even 7-Elevens often offer espresso coffee as a carryout.

The interest in gourmet coffees has evolved over the years. The latest craze is *cafe latte*, which is espresso mixed with lots of frothy milk, more so than a simple cappuccino.

Seattle has scores of tiny bistros serving only coffee, but the choices offered in even the tiniest shop make a stop a wonderful experience. You must decide whether you wish your *cafe latte* to be short, tall, or grande. This indicates how much milk is put into the coffee. Next, you must decide whether you wish a single, double, or triple espresso. The last items to decide on are what type of milk you wish—nonfat, 2 percent fat, or whole—and decaf or regular coffee. You can also get regular coffee (hold the milk), plain espresso, or cappuccino. Some of the cafes also have pastries and other temptations.

In Portland, Marco's Cafe and Espresso Bar at 7910 SW 35th Avenue (503/245–0199) is a great espresso stop as well

The heart and soul of Vancouver is Robson Street, Vancouver's version of the Champs Elysee. Robson Street (affectionately called Robsonstrasse by city residents) is a busy boulevard day and night—a great place for walks, window-shopping, and people-watching.

Start your tour at Robson Square, at Robson and Howe streets. This outdoor park combines government offices with concrete plazas, and the renovated 1912 courthouse that is home to the Vancouver Art Gallery, with a fine collection of paintings by as a fine restaurant. In Vancouver, B.C., coffee houses can be found along Robson Street. One of our favorites is the Milieu Cafe at 1145 Robson, a cappuccino bar and patisserie on the first level and a trendy restaurant on the second. Seattle, of course, has far too many to list, but here is a sampling of some around that town:

**Allegro Cafe**—4214 University Way NE, 206/633–3030.

**Botticelli**—101 Stewart Street, 206/441–9235.

**Burke Museum Cafe**—(also known as The Boiserie) inside the Burke Museum at the University of Washington, 17th Avenue NE and NE 45th Street, 206/543–5590.

**Cafe Counter Intelligence**—94 Pike Place, Suite 32 in the Corner Market Building, 206/622–6979.

**La Tazz di Caffe**—1503 Queen Anne Avenue N, 206/284–8984.

**M. Coy Books and Espresso**—117 Pine Street, 206/623–5354.

**Starbucks**—1912 Pike Place. This is the original store; there are 35 newer ones throughout the city. 206/448–8762.

**Torrefazione Italia**—320 Occidental Avenue S, 206/624–5773 and 622 Olive Way, 206/624–5773.

**Uptown Espresso**—525 Queen Anne Avenue N, 206/281–8669.

Canadian artist Emily Carr and works by American, Canadian, and European artists from the seventeenth-century to the present.

Outside this square, eclectic shops are the real masters. There are so many stores that it is easy to get the impression that the major activity in Vancouver is shopping. Stroll along Robson Street from the square west to the 1200 block to experience this wonderful array of offerings. Here you can buy Indian arts and crafts at Fitzcrombie's Fine Arts at 1167 Robson Street, at Images for a Canadian Heritage, just off Robson at 779 Burrard Street, and at Silver Blue Traders, at 1165 Robson Street. Mixed in with these fine Native American shops are scores of upscale boutiques for both men and women, sidewalk cafes, shoe shops, art galleries, an occasional antique store, coffee shops, and fine restaurants.

More shops are found on the cross streets and the major paralleling corridors of Georgia and Dunsmuir streets, as well as in the new Pacific Centre (200 shops at West Georgia and Granville streets), the four renovated government buildings that make the Sinclair Centre (scores of shops at Hastings and Howe streets), the Vancouver Centre Mall (20 very chic boutiques at 650 West Georgia Street), and The Landing, a chic shopping mall at 375 Water Street. (The unusual white-top waterfront building west of The Landing is the Canada Place Pier, where the cruise ships dock. Canada Place's gleaming white fabric roof makes it look like a cross between a huge circus tent and a tall sailing ship.)

The Landing mall is at the entrance to Gastown, Vancouver's former warehouse and flophouse district that has now been turned into a district of antique shops, funky boutiques, restaurants, nightclubs, and galleries.

Formed in 1867, Gastown got its name from "Gassy" Jack Deighton, the first saloon keeper in the town. A statue of Gassy Jack, probably as stiff now as he was in life, stands in a tiny park at Maple Tree Square. The shops and attractions line Powell, Water, Alexander, Columbia, and Cordova streets in this wonderful area.

You can find good athletic wear at the Pacific Short Co. at 154 Water Street, contemporary fashions and Vancouver items at Suraj Fashions & Gifts at 339 Water Street, Native American crafts at Hill's Indian Crafts at 185 Water Street, and souvenirs at Steam Clock T-Shirts at 305 Water Street. This last shop is named after an unusual Gastown landmark, the Steam Clock at Water and Cambie streets. The steam-powered clock sounds off the hours with chimes and a puff of steam.

Gastown is just one of Vancouver's fascinating neighborhoods. Three blocks east of Gassy Jack's statue is North America's second largest Chinatown (San Francisco's is the largest). This Chinatown, centered around Pender and Keefer streets between Gore and Carrall streets, was created in the late 1800s by the huge number of immigrants brought over to work on the Canadian Pacific Railway.

Amid the beehive of shops, herbalists, acupuncture clinics, restaurants, food vendors, and tacky gift shops is the interesting Chinese Cultural Center and the beautiful Dr. Sun Yat-Sen Garden; both at 578 Carrall Street. The garden is in classic Ming style and was built by landscape artists from the People's Republic of China. It is the first classic Chinese garden built outside that nation.

Other attractions lie west, north, and south of downtown Vancouver. To the west is Stanley Park, a 1,000-acre sanctuary with lovely landscaped gardens, totem poles, a swimming pool, sand beaches, a marina, a golf course, tennis courts, a zoo, and a magnificent aquarium. A visit here is a must. You can rent bicycles at the vendor near the park entrance on West Georgia Street. You must ride your bikes in a counterclockwise direction in the park, and signs will direct you to bike paths.

As you take the waterfront Scenic Drive you come to the turnoffs for the zoo and aquarium and then a small causeway leading to Deadman's Island, a former Indian burial ground and now a small naval base. On the island is the Nine O'Clock Gun, which fires to signal that hour each evening. Past the causeway on the spit of land called Brockton Point is the park containing imposing totem poles carved by the Haida and Kwakiutl Indians.

Continuing around the park, you pass by a replica of the SS Empress of Japan figurehead (the ship was a trading vessel), go under the Lions Gate Bridge, and then reach Prospect Point, a haven for cormorants and blue herons. Continue past the point and you come to the Seawall Promenade turnoff to the left. Take it and go to English Bay and the park's sand beaches. The Ferguson Point Teahouse on the seawall is a popular place for lunch. The views are great and the location in the forest-flanked meadow is serene. The Seawall Promenade continues around the park, returning to merge with the Scenic Drive and eventually exit back to downtown Vancouver.

South of downtown is Granville Island, a renovated industrial island that features an inn, a sprawling public market, numerous art galleries and studios with works in progress, theaters, the Emily Carr College of Art and Design, marinas and a ship's store, a Kids Only Market, a brewery, and a cement factory. The island has wonderful views of downtown Vancouver and is the site of many fun-filled festivals.

Finding your way around the island can be confusing. Stop by the information center at the entrance to the public market and pick up the map and brochure about the shops. Some must-stops include the Granville Island Brewery, the Indian crafts at the Cartwright Gallery, the gifts at the Net Loft, the Circle Crafts Co-operative, the Asian baskets and carvings at Rhinoceros, and the contemporary arts at the Wickaninnish Gallery.

For nightlife, the Waterfront Theatre on the island often books shows that sold out in their first runs at the bigger theaters in town.

You can reach the island by driving over the Granville bridge or—a better way—by taking the cute False Creek Ferries that shuttle from the dock at the foot of Thurlow Street in downtown Vancouver to the island's marina. The ferries depart every six minutes, and the short journey manages to offer a closeup look at the fine hotels, marinas, yachts, and apartment buildings on False Creek.

More attractions are found in south Vancouver, beyond Granville Island. Here you will find the Vancouver Museum, the Maritime Museum, and the H.R. MacMillan Planetarium at 1100 Chestnut Street. The Vancouver Museum has exhibits of decorative arts, Northwest Indian culture, and Vancouver history; the Maritime Museum celebrates explorers and the sea; and the planetarium offers a tour of the night sky. Other museums and attractions in south Vancouver include the University of British Columbia's fine Botanical Garden at 6250 SW Marine Drive, a display that has a wonderful Japanese tea garden, Alpine Garden, and food garden; the UBC Museum of Anthropology at Point Grey Cliffs has a massive exhibit of Northwest Indian artifacts as well as collections from Africa and Asia.

North of town are more scenic destinations. The Capilano Suspension Bridge and Park has displays of totem poles and a 450-foot-long swaying suspension bridge that is 230 feet over a deep ravine. It is incredibly breathtaking to take the walk over the swaying bridge. The bridge is on North Capilano Road and follows the Capilano River. North of the bridge is the Capilano Fish Hatchery, where you can see salmon climbing a fish ladder on their way upstream.

At the top of Capilano Road is Grouse Mountain, which offers some stunning views of Vancouver from its 4,100-foot-high summit. You can ski in the winter, ride a hay wagon or a helicopter, see a multimedia show about Vancouver, or just enjoy a meal. The aerial tramway runs year-round to the summit chalet for the views of the city below. By day or night, it is an amazing sight.

For longer daytrips out of Vancouver, consider a visit to Whistler Resort. This year-round resort offers the two busiest ski mountains on the continent—Whistler and Blackcomb. The skiing is great in winter months, but only passable in the summer, although you may want to try skiing on a glacier.

Whistler village has more than a score of inns and hotels, fine shops, good restaurants, and a world of interesting distractions. The adjacent Garibaldi Provincial Forest is a 78,000-acre wilderness with fishing, hiking, and biking trails.

## For More Information

**Edmonton—Edmonton Convention and Tourism Authority,** 1049797 Jasper Avenue, Edmonton, AB T5J 1N9. 403/988–5455. Other Edmonton information centers are at 97th Street and Jasper Avenue and at the Edmonton International Airport.

**Portland—Portland/Oregon Visitors Association,** 26 SW Salmon Street, Portland, OR 97204. 503/222–2223.

**Seattle—Seattle/King County Convention & Visitors Bureau,** 520 Pike Street, Suite 1300, Seattle, WA 98101. 206/461–5840.

**Vancouver—Vancouver Travel Infocentre,** 1055 Dunsmuir Street, Box 49296, Vancouver, BC V7X 1L3. 604/683–2000

## *Where and When*

### *In Edmonton:*

**Edmonton Art Gallery**—2 Sir Winston Churchill Square. Open 10:30 AM to 5:00 PM Monday through Wednesday; 10:30 AM to 8:00 PM Thursday and Friday; 11:00 AM to 5:00 PM Saturday and Sunday. 403/422–6223.

**Edmonton Space & Science Center**—142 Street and 112 Avenue. Open 10:00 AM to 10:00 PM Sunday through Thursday; 10:00 AM to midnight Friday and Saturday. 403/451–7722.

**Fort Edmonton Park**—Whitemud Drive and Fox Drive. Open 10:00 AM to 6:00 PM daily. 403/428–2992.

**John Janzen Nature Centre**—Off Whitemud Drive near Fort Edmonton Park. Open 9:00 AM to 6:00 PM weekdays; 11:00 AM to 6:00 PM weekends. 403/428–7900.

**Muttgart Conservatory**—98 Avenue and 96A Street. Open 11:00 AM to 9:00 PM daily in the summer; 11:00 AM to 6:00 PM daily the rest of the year. 403/428–5226.

**Provincial Museum of Alberta**—12845 102 Avenue. Open 9:00 AM to 8:00 PM daily during the summer; 9:00 AM to 5:00 PM Tuesday through Sunday the rest of the year. 403/453–9100.

**Rutherford House**—11153 Saskatchewan Drive. Open 10:00 AM to 6:00 PM daily in the summer; noon to 5:00 PM daily the rest of the year. 403/427–2022.

**Ukrainian Canadian Archives & Museum**—9543 110 Avenue. Open 1:00 PM to 5:00 PM Monday through Saturday May through September 1; 1:00 PM to 4:00 PM Tuesday through Saturday the rest of the year. 403/424–7580.

**Ukrainian Cultural Heritage Village**—Thirty-one miles east of town on Highway 16. Open 10:00 AM to 6:00 PM daily in the summer; 10:00 AM to 4:00 PM weekdays the rest of the year. 403/662–3640.

**Ukrainian Museum of Canada**—10611 110 Avenue. Open 8:00 AM to 4:00 PM Monday through Friday; 2:00 PM to 5:00 PM Sunday from June through August, by appointment only the rest of the year. 403/466–4216.

**West Edmonton Mall**—87 Avenue and 170 Street. Open 10:00 AM to 10:00 PM Monday through Saturday; 10:00 AM to 8:00 PM Sunday. Free shuttle buses run between the mall and most major hotels. 403/444–5200.

## In the Portland Area:

**Columbia Gorge**—Stern-wheeler offering river cruises out of Marine Park in Cascade Locks. Three departures daily in the summer. 503/223–3928.

**Ft. Vancouver**—612 E Reserve Street, Vancouver, WA. Open 10:00 AM to 4:00 PM daily. 206/696–7655.

**Hoyt Arboretum**—4000 SW Fairview Boulevard. Open dawn to dusk daily. 503/228–8732.

**International Rose Test Garden**—400 SW Kingston Avenue. Open dawn to dusk daily. 503/796–5193.

**Japanese Gardens**—On SW Kingston Avenue in Washington Park, next to the Rose Gardens. Open 10:00 AM to 6:00 PM daily April through September; 10:00 AM to 4:00 PM daily the rest of year. 503/223–4070.

**Maryhill Museum**—35 Maryhill Museum Drive, Maryhill, WA. Open 9:00 AM to 5:00 PM daily March 15 to November 15. 509/773–3733.

**New Market Theater Village**—50 SW Second Avenue. Open 10:00 AM to 6:00 PM daily. 503/228–2392.

**Oregon Art Institute (and Portland Art Museum)**—1219 SW Park Avenue. Open 11:00 AM to 5:00 PM Tuesday through Saturday; 1:00 PM to 5:00 PM Sunday. 503/221–1156.

**Oregon Historical Society**—1230 SW Park Avenue. Open 10:00 AM to 4:45 PM Monday through Saturday. 503/222–1741.

**Oregon Maritime Museum**—113 SW Front Street. Open 11:00 AM to 4:00 PM Friday through Sunday. 503/224-7724.

**Pittock Mansion**—3229 NW Pittock Drive. Open 1:00 PM to 5:00 PM daily. 503/248-4469.

**Portland Center for the Performing Arts**—1111 SW Broadway Avenue. Call for performance schedule. 503/248-4496.

**Portland Saturday Market**—100 SW Ankeny Street. Open 10:00 AM to 5:00 PM Saturday; 11:00 AM to 4:30 PM Sunday March through December. 503/222-6072.

**Skidmore Fountain Building**—28 SW First Avenue. Open 10:00 AM to 6:00 PM daily. 503/227-5305.

**Washington Park Zoo**—4001 SW Canyon Road. Open 9:00 AM to 6:00 PM daily during the summer; 9:00 AM to 4:30 PM daily the rest of year. 503/226-ROAR.

**World Forestry Center**—4033 SW Canyon Road. Open 9:00 AM to 5:00 PM daily during the summer; 10:00 AM to 5:00 PM daily the rest of the year. 503/228-1367.

**Yamhill Marketplace**—111 SW Yamhill Street. Open 7:00 AM to 7:00 PM weekdays; 7:30 AM to 6:00 PM Saturday; 10:00 AM to 6:00 PM Sunday. 503/224-6705.

## *In Seattle:*

**Chateau Ste. Michelle**—1411 NE 145th Street, Woodinville. Open 10:00 AM to 4:30 PM daily except holidays. 206/488-1133.

**Columbia Winery**—14030 NE 145th Street, Woodinville. Open 10:00 AM to 5:00 PM daily. 206/488-2776.

**Henry Art Gallery**—15th Avenue NE and NE 41st Street. Open 10:00 AM to 5:00 PM Tuesday through Friday; 10:00 AM to 7:00 PM Thursday; and 11:00 AM to 5:00 PM weekends. Closed Mondays. 206/543-2280.

**Hiram M. Chittenden Locks**—3015 NW 54th Street, west of the Ballard Bridge. Visitors' center open 10:00 AM to 7:00 PM daily; closed in winter months. 206/783-7059.

**Kingdome**—201 S King Street. Call for performance schedule. 206/296-3111.

**Klondike Gold Rush National Historic Park Visitors'
Center**—117 S Main Street, Pioneer Square. Open 9:00 AM to
5:00 PM daily. 206/442-7220.

**Monorail**—Westlake Center to Seattle Center. Runs 9:00 AM
to 9:00 PM Sunday through Thursday; 9:00 AM to midnight Friday
and Saturday. 206/684-7200.

**Museum of History and Industry**—2700 24th Avenue E.
Open 10:00 AM to 5:00 PM daily. 206/324-1125.

**Museum of Flight**—9404 E Marginal Way S. Open 10:00
AM to 5:00 PM Monday, Wednesday, Friday, and Sunday; 10:00
AM to 9:00 PM Thursday. 206/764-5720.

**Nippon Kan Theater**—628 S Washington Street. Call for
performance schedule. 206/624-8800.

**Northwest Crafts Center**—Seattle Center. Open 11:00 AM
to 6:00 PM Tuesday through Sunday. 206/728-1555.

**Omnidome Film Experience**—Pier 59. Open 10:00 AM to
5:00 PM daily. 206/622-1868.

**Pike Place Market**—First Avenue at Pike Street. Open 9:00
AM to 6:00 PM Monday through Saturday. 206/682-7453.

**Seattle Aquarium**—Pier 59. Open 10:00 AM to 5:00 PM
daily. 206/386-4320.

**Seattle Art Museum**—1320 Second Avenue. Open 10:00
AM to 5:00 PM Tuesday through Saturday (closes at 9:00 PM Thursday); noon to 5:00 PM Sunday. 206/625-8989.

**Seattle Harbor Tours**—Pier 55. Up to six tours daily, depending on the time of year. 206/623-1445.

**Space Needle**—Seattle Center. Open 8:00 AM to 1:00 AM
daily in the summer; 10:00 AM to midnight daily the rest of year.
206/443-2111.

**Stena Line**—Pier 48. Daily round trips to Victoria, B.C. for
passengers and vehicles. 206/624-6986 and 604/388-7397.

**Thomas Burke Memorial Washington State Museum**—
17th Avenue NE and NE 45th Street. Open 10:00 AM to 5:00 PM
(closes at 8:00 PM Thursday). 206/543-5590.

**Tillicum Village Tours**—Pier 56. Up to three four-hour
tours a day, depending on the time of year. 206/443-1244.

**Underground Seattle Tours**—Doc Maynard's Public House, 610 First Avenue. Tours daily (not handicapped-accessible). 206/682-4646.

**Victoria Clipper**—Pier 69. Two to three departures daily, depending on the time of year. 206/448-5000 and 800/888-2535.

**Washington Park Arboretum**—2300 Arboretum Drive E. Open 7:00 AM to sunset daily. 206/325-4510.

**Washington State Ferry System**—Pier 52. Numerous departures daily. 206/464-6400 and 800/542-7052.

**Wing Luke Museum**—407 Seventh Avenue S. Open 11:00 AM to 4:30 PM Tuesday through Friday; noon to 4:00 PM weekends. 206/623-5124.

## In Vancouver:

**Capilano Fish Hatchery**—4500 Capilano Park Road. Open 8:00 AM to 8:00 PM daily. 604/987-1411.

**Capilano Suspension Bridge and Park**—Capilano Road, North Vancouver. Open 8:00 AM to 9:30 PM daily in the summer, hours vary the rest of the year. 604/985-7474.

**Dr. Sun Yat-Sen Garden**—578 Carrall Street. Open 10:00 AM to 8:00 PM daily May through September; 10:00 AM to 4:30 PM October through April. 604/689-7133.

**Granville Island Brewery**—1441 Cartwright Street, Granville Island. Tours at 2:00 PM weekdays; at 1:00 PM and 3:00 PM Sundays. 604/688-9927.

**Granville Island Information Center**—1592 Johnston Street. Open 10:00 AM to 6:00 PM daily. 604/666-5784.

**Grouse Mountain**—6400 Nancy Greene Way, at north end of Capilano Road. Park and aerial tramway open 9:00 AM to 10:00 PM daily. 604/984-0661.

**H.R. McMillan Planetarium**—1100 Chestnut Street. Call for show times. 604/736-4431.

**Maritime Museum**—1100 Chestnut Street. Open 10:00 AM to 5:00 PM daily. 604/737-2211.

**Stanley Park**—At west end of Georgia Avenue. The park is open daily. Call 604/683-3525. The Aquarium and Zoo are open

9:30 AM to 8:00 PM daily in the summer; 10:00 AM to 5:30 PM the rest of the year. 604/682–1118.

**UBC Botanical Garden—**6250 SW Marine Drive. Open at 10:00 AM daily, closing times vary. 604/228–4804.

**UBC Museum of Anthropology—**Point Grey Cliffs. Open 11:00 AM to 9:00 PM Tuesday; 11:00 AM to 5:00 PM Wednesday through Sunday. 604/228–5807.

**Vancouver Art Gallery—**750 Hornby Street. Open 10:00 AM to 5:00 PM Monday, Wednesday, Friday, and Saturday; 10:00 AM to 9:00 PM Thursday; noon to 5:00 PM Sunday; open Tuesdays during the summer (call for hours). 604/682–4668.

**Vancouver Museum—**1100 Chestnut Street. Open 10:00 AM to 5:00 PM daily, Victoria Day (May 24th or closest Monday) through Labour Day; 10:00 AM to 5:00 PM Tuesday through Sunday the rest of the year. 604/736–4431.

**Whistler Resort—**Open year-round. 604/685–3650 from Vancouver; 800/634–9622 from the United States. Whistler Travel Infocentre, 604/932–5528.

## Romantic Retreats

Here are our favorite places to stay and dine. But first, an explanation of our cost categories:

One night in a hotel, resort, or inn for two:

*Inexpensive*—Less than $75.
*Moderate*—$75 to $125.
*Expensive*—More than $125.

Dinner for two (wine and drinks not included):

*Inexpensive*—Less than $25.
*Moderate*—$25 to $50.
*Expensive*—More than $50.

## *Romantic Lodging in Edmonton:*

**Chateau Lacombe—**This is a stunning 24-story white tower that offers 317 rooms and suites, all tastefully decorated. The view is great, particularly at night when the lights on the river and the city glow below. Moderate. 10111 Bellamy Hill, Edmonton, AB T5J 1N7. 403/428–6611, 800/268–9411 (in Alberta), 800/828–7447 in the United States.

**La Bohème—**This historic building is more famous as a fine French restaurant than as an inn. This B&B has eight suites, with one or two bedrooms. Each suite is stylishly decorated. Moderate. 6427 112 Avenue, Edmonton, AB T5W 0N9. 403/474–5693.

**Westin Hotel—**This massive yet beautiful hotel sits atop a shopping plaza and offers 416 spacious and contemporary rooms, a fantastic lobby, a swimming pool, whirlpool, and sauna. Moderate (inexpensive on weekends). 10135 100 Street, Edmonton, AB T5J 0N7. 403/426–3636, 800/228–3000.

## *Fine Dining in Edmonton:*

**Bistro La Bodega—**Excellent continental cuisine served in a restaurant with the finest wine bar in Edmonton. Go on weekends when chef Jurg Weber offers his most creative dishes. Expensive. 10165 104 Street. 403/423–0679.

**Cafe Budapest—**Gypsy steak, chicken paprika, and kettle goulash are the stars at this cozy cafe. Moderate. 10145 104 Street. 403/426–4363.

**Geppetto's—**First-rate Italian fare served in a lovely, plant-filled dining room. Moderate. 10162 100A Street. 403/426–1635.

**La Bohème—**This historic building is an elegant B&B as well as an outstanding French restaurant. The specialty is seafood, served in an Old World atmosphere. Outdoor dining available. Expensive. 6427 112 Avenue. 403/474–5693.

**La Spiga—**This northern Italian restaurant is located in a mansion built in 1915. The house specialty is a wonderful rack of lamb. Outdoor dining available, but the mansion rooms are fabulous. Expensive. 10133 125 Street. 403/482–3100.

**Mother Tucker's Food Experience**—A casual atmosphere and hearty homestyle cooking make this a real treat. Inexpensive. 10184 104 Street. 403/424-0351.

**Shogun**—You will have an interesting and entertaining dinner at this classic Japanese seafood/beef/poultry house, whose chef is also a trained juggler. Moderate. 121 Street and Jasper Avenue. 403/482-5494.

**Unheardof**—Offers a prix fixe menu, with only two dinner options; either will be outstanding, but call first to see if they suit you. 9602 82 Avenue. 403/432-0480.

## Romantic Lodging in Portland:

**Columbia Gorge Hotel**—Located 60 miles east of Portland in the Columbia River Gorge town of Hood River, this three-story inn offers 42 spacious rooms filled with antiques and reproductions. Some rooms have fireplaces. The grounds are lovely, with a grand 13-acre garden and a pleasant creek. Expensive. 4000 W Cliff Drive, Hood River, OR 97031. 503/386-5566, 800/345-1921.

**Heathman Hotel**—This historic hotel is the center of Portland's political, social, and economic life. There are 152 rooms, all very tastefully decorated in soft greens, roses, and creams. Don't miss afternoon tea or a drink in the stunning marble bar. Expensive. 1009 SW Broadway, Portland, OR 97205. 503/241-4100, 800/551-0011.

**John Palmer House**—This magnificently restored 1890 Victorian is a true delight. There are two suites and a room in the main house and two more rooms in the cottage. For a very romantic getaway, reserve the Bridal Suite, which has its own library, porch, and sitting area. The furnishings are antiques and are outstanding. Moderate. 4314 N Mississippi Avenue, Portland, OR 97217. 503/284-5893.

**MacMaster House**—The mansion offers seven fireplaces, works by local artists, and six nicely appointed guest rooms. Two of the rooms have fireplaces. Great location on the park. Moderate. 1041 SW Vista Avenue, Portland, OR 97205. 503/223-7362.

**Mumford Manor**—This newly restored Queen Anne offers three tastefully decorated rooms and one lavish Victorian suite with a fireplace. Moderate. 1130 SW King Avenue, Portland, OR 97205. 503/243-2443.

**Portland's White House**—This white Doric-columned mansion was built in 1910 entirely from Honduran mahagony imported by a timber baron. Unlike some old mansions, this B&B has retained the touches of wealth: a circular driveway, massive chandeliers, a carriage house, and fountain. There are six spacious rooms filled with antiques and oriental rugs. Moderate. 1914 NE 22nd Avenue, Portland, OR 97212. 503/287-7131.

**River Place Alexis Hotel**—This very chic waterfront hotel is as elegant as its twin in Seattle. There are 74 rooms and ten apartments, all very carefully furnished with contemporary pieces. Ask for a room facing the Willamette River. Expensive. 1510 SW Harbor Way, Portland, OR 97201. 503/228-3233.

**Westin Benson**—More than 80 years old, this fine hotel still offers style and elegance. There are 320 rooms, with the ones in the original hotel a bit too small for comfort, yet tastefully furnished. The rooms in the new section are larger and more contemporary. Expensive. 309 SW Broadway, Portland, OR 97205. 503/228-2000, 800/228-3000.

**Williams House**—This elegant, 1899 light-green Victorian in The Dalles in the Columbia River Gorge is stunning. The inn offers three rooms, two of which have private porches with views of the Klickitat Hills. Moderate. 608 W Sixth Street, The Dalles, OR 97058. 503/296-2889.

## *Fine Dining in Portland:*

**Atwater's**—The view from the 30th floor of the U.S. Bancorp Tower is so sensational that you may forget that the view on the plate in front of you is also ousatanding. Northwest cuisine is the fare, featuring local seafood, venison, and other game. Expensive. 111 SW Fifth Avenue. 503/275-3600.

**L'Auberge**—This is a superb restaurant with a split personality. In the main dining room some of the finest French dishes in the Pacific Northwest are served each evening. In the rustic upstairs bar, suprisingly creative seafood, salads, and light fare are served. And on Sunday nights, cheeseburgers and great BBQ ribs are doled out, along with screenings of some classic old films. Expensive. 2601 NW Vaughn Street. 503/223–3302.

**Cafe des Amis**—Hearty stews from France and the Pyrenees, perhaps the best steaks in town, and excellent seafood make this cafe a special find. Moderate. 1987 NW Kearny Street. 503/295–6487.

**Couch Street Fish House**—Continental cuisine is served here in a beautiful dining room filled with watercolors, antiques, and plants, in a building that dates to 1873. Expensive. 105 NW Third Avenue. 503/223–6173.

**Digger O'Dell's Oyster Bar**—Located in a century-old theater, this elegant restaurant serves an extensive Cajun menu in a room that's as heavy on the red velvet as the food is on the spices. Moderate. 532 SE Grand Avenue. 503/238–6996.

**Eddie Lee's**—Innovative cuisine, with an emphasis on seafood in a casual but chic dining room. Inexpensive. 409 SW Second Street. 503/228–1874.

**Esplanade At River Place**—The riverfront setting makes this dining room very romantic. The cuisine is innovative Northwestern, emphasizing fresh local seafood prepared with some French accents. Expensive. In the Riverplace Alexis Hotel, 1510 SW Harbor Way. 503/295–6166.

**Genoa**—Northern Italian food that is sensational. The intimate dining room is barely lit, the courses plentiful, and the boccono dolce of meringue, berries, chocolate, and cream worth dying for. Moderate. 2832 SE Belmont Street. 503/238–1464.

**Grant House**—The innovative seafood and game dishes are as elegant as the dining room at this Vancouver, Washington restaurant. The former president and Civil War general ate many meals here. Expensive. 1101 Officers' Row, Vancoucer, WA. 206/696–9699.

**The Heathman Restaurant**—Long acclaimed as the showcase of Northwest Cuisine, this excellent restaurant in the Heathman Hotel offers outstanding innovative seafood and game dishes. Expensive. 1009 SW Broadway. 503/241–4100.

**Indigine**—For something different, try Saturday night at this casual cafe, when the menu is East Indian. Weeknights? Perhaps Central American, Pacific Northwest, or even European, all with a special flair. Moderate. 3725 SE Division Street. 503/238–1470.

**Rheinlander**—Singing waiters, strolling musicians, Bavarian kitsch, fondues, sauerbrauten, roast pork, and wurst. You get the idea. It's lots of fun. Moderate. 5035 NW Sandy Boulevard. 503/288–5503.

## *Romantic Lodging in Seattle:*

**Alexis Hotel**—This renovated circa-1900 building offers 54 stylish rooms near the waterfront and lots of quiet elegance. One caution: there are no views of the water, so ask for a room overlooking the center courtyard. The suites have fireplaces and jacuzzis. Expensive. 1007 First Avenue, Seattle, WA 98104. 206/624–4844, 800/426–7033.

**Beech Tree Manor**—This 1904 mansion on Queen Anne Hill offers four beautifully decorated bedrooms as well as an impressive collection of abstract art. Inexpensive. 1405 Queen Anne Avenue N, Seattle, WA 98109. 206/281–7037.

**Chambered Nautilus**—This classic colonial sits on a hill in Seattle's University district. There are six guest rooms, each spacious and nicely furnished. Moderate. 5005 22nd Avenue NE, Seattle, WA 98105. 206/522–2536.

**Four Seasons Olympic**—The grand dame of Seattle hotels has been renovated and glows once again. All 450 rooms have a new decor and lighting. The grand lobby and elegant Palm Room are worth a visit even if you don't stay here. Expensive. 411 University Street, Seattle, WA 98101. 206/621–1700, 800/223–8772.

**Gaslight Inn**—This circa-1900 mansion offers eight guest rooms, each decorated differently but stylishly, and is a very warm and friendly B&B. Moderate. 1727 15th Avenue, Seattle, WA 98122. 206/325–3654.

**Inn at the Market**—This small hotel offers 65 spacious rooms, built around a central courtyard in the Pike Place Market. Expensive. 86 Pine Street, Seattle, WA 98101. 206/443–3600, 800/446–4484.

**Seattle Sheraton**—This luxurious, modern hotel is superbly located—across from City Centre, a few blocks from Nordstrom's and a ten-minute walk to the Pike Place Market. The 840 rooms are spacious, very comfortable, and offer great views of the city and surrounding countryside. Expensive. 1400 Sixth Avenue, Seattle, WA 98101. 206/621–9000, 800/325–3535.

**Sorrento Hotel**—Once the grandest hotel in town, the Sorrento faded and then was reborn. This Renaissance-style structure offers 76 rooms tastefully decorated with an oriental flair. Ask for a corner suite if you want a great view of Puget Sound. Expensive. 900 Madison Street, Seattle, WA 98104. 206/622–6400, 800/426–1265.

**Westin Hotel**—This twin-tower hotel offers spacious rooms and outstanding views from the upper floors. Facilities include a pool and exercise room. Expensive. 1900 Fifth Avenue, Seattle, WA 98101. 206/728–1000, 800/228–3000.

## Fine Dining in Seattle:

**Adriatica**—This hillside house requires you work up an appetite by first climbing a long staircase. Once there you will find a menu featuring dishes from Greece, Italy, Yugoslavia, and France (which is one nation away from the Adriatic). Despite the lack of geographical loyalty, the cooking here is superb. Expensive. 1107 Dexter Avenue N. 206/285–5000.

**Botticelli Cafe**—This fantastic four-table aperitif bar offers tasty lunch fare. Stop by in the midafternoon for a salad, some bread and pesto, or a light sandwich. Inexpensive. 101 Stewart Street. 206/441–9235.

**Cafe Alexis**—Innovative Northwestern cuisine, with an emphasis on game and seafood, served in an elegant, yet cozy cafe. Expensive. In the Alexis Hotel, 1007 First Avenue. 206/624–3646.

**Cafe Sport**—The decor is minimalist but this cafe/bar offers a wonderfully creative marriage of Pacific Rim and Northwest cuisine. It's superb! Moderate. 2020 Western Avenue. 206/443–6000.

**Chez Shea**—Candlelit tables, windows facing the Sound, and a four-course prix-fixe menu offering seafood and game dishes add up to a romantic and sensational dining room. Expensive. Suite 34, Corner Market Building, Pike Place Market. 206/467–9990.

**Dominique's**—Outstanding French cuisine, featuring fresh seafood, crepes, game, and meal-size salads. Chef/owner Dominique Place features four- and five-course prix fixe dinners. The restaurant has views of Lake Washington and the Cascades. Expensive. 1927 43rd Avenue E. 206/329–6620.

**Fuller's**—As fine a hotel restaurant as you can find, with chef Caprial Pence always surprising you with her version of Northwest and Pacific Rim cuisine. The creative cuisine is served in an art-filled dining room that, despite its size, remains intimate because of the subdued lighting. Expensive. In the Seattle Sheraton, 1400 Sixth Avenue. 206/447–5544.

**Georgian Room**—The most ornate and elegant dining room in town, featuring huge chandeliers, towering potted palms, and white-glove service. The cuisine is continental with Northwestern touches. Expensive. In the Four Seasons Olympic Hotel, 411 University Street. 206/621–7889.

**Hunt Club**—Nouvelle cuisine, with an emphasis on local seafood, served in a dignified, clublike setting. Expensive. In the Sorrento Hotel, 900 Madison Street. 206/622–6400.

**Labuznik**—Hearty eastern European fare, focusing on such standards as roast duck or pork, rack of lamb, and chops. Expensive. 1924 First Avenue. 206/441–8899.

**Le Gourmand**—This small French bistro serves a prix fixe menu featuring whatever is in season and fresh that day. Expensive. 425 NW Market Street. 206/784–3463.

**Le Tastevin**—Traditional French cuisine, tempered by American health consciousness and a Northwestern flair. Expensive. 19 W Harrison Street. 206/283–0991.

**Lombardi's Cucina**—This busy and often noisy Italian dining room in Ballard near the locks serves outstanding classic Italian dishes. Moderate. 2200 NW Market Street. 206/783–0055.

**Pink Door**—This indoor/outdoor spot near Pike Place Market serves excellent Italian cuisine. Go on a warm night, when you can dine out on the rooftop garden. There is live entertainment on many weekend evenings. Moderate. 1919 Post Alley. 206/443–3241.

**Rover's**—Fine French/Northwestern cuisine. We enjoyed dining outdoors in the garden. Moderate. 2808 E Madison Street. 206/325–7442.

**Saleh al Lago**—Outstanding Middle Eastern cuisine with an Italian accent. The veal dishes and pastas have the starring roles. Expensive. 6804 E Green Lake. 206/522–7943.

**Wild Ginger**—Pacific Rim cuisine, with a definite lean toward Chinese, Vietnamese, and Thai cooking. The decor is more like that of a pub—dark wood, high-backed booths—but the food is sensational and the daily specials are marvelous. Moderate. 1400 Western Avenue. 206/623–4450.

## *Romantic Lodging in Vancouver:*

**Delta Place**—Once the most expensive hotel in town, this incredibly luxurious hotel has changed owners, cut its prices, and enjoyed a new popularity. The 459 rooms are still plush, and the facilities include three pools, whirlpool, sauna, indoor tennis, and more. Expensive. 645 How Street, Vancouver, BC V6C 2Y9. 604/687–1122, 800/268–1133.

**Four Seasons**—We usually don't like hotels attached to shopping centers, even when they are as luxurious as this 385-room hotel attached to the upscale Pacific Centre. But we admit that the rooms are plush, the public areas even more luxurious, and the shopping is, well, right outside your door. Expensive. 791 W Georgia Street, Vancouver, BC V6C 2T4. 604/689–9333, 800/268–6282.

**Granville Island Hotel**—If the focus of your visit is the art galleries and shops on Granville Island, or if you want a quiet island retreat away from the metropolitan area, catch the small, cute ferry for this 54-room hotel that combines a renovated old stucco building with a modernistic new glass, metal, and concrete addition. The rooms are pleasantly furnished, and some have balconies. Expensive. At 1253 Johnston Street, Vancouver, BC V6H 3R9. 604/683–7373, 800/663–1840.

**Hotel Vancouver**—The majestic chateau-style hotel commands the center of downtown Vancouver. There are 466 rooms and 42 suites. The suites on the Entré Gold floors are spacious, beautifully furnished, and are a throwback to the days of style and class. The rooms on the other floors are pleasant, but not special. Facilities include a health club and pool. Expensive. 900 W Georgia Street, Vancouver, BC V6C 2W6. 604/684–3131, 800/ 268–9143 in western Canada.

**Le Meridien**—This elegant hotel near the Vancouver Art Museum offers 397 spacious rooms, some of which have the best views in town. The hotel has a fitness club, pool, and a beautiful and dramatic lobby. Expensive. 845 Burrard Street, Vancouver, BC V6Z 2K6. 604/682–5511, 800/543–4300.

**Pacific Palisades**—There are 233 nicely appointed rooms and suites in this recently renovated hotel. The location on the west end of Robson Street is excellent, putting you close to the shops as well as the waterfront and Stanley Park. The indoor pool and exercise room overlook a lovely and tranquil Japanese garden. Expensive. 1277 Robson Street, Vancouver, BC V6E 1C4. 604/688–0461, 800/663–1815.

**Pan Pacific Hotel**—The great, white hotel is part of Canada Place. It has 505 rooms, some offering striking views of the harbor and Stanley Park. Rooms are small, though. Expensive. 300-999 Canada Place, Vancouver, BC V6C 3B5. 604/662–8111, 800/ 937–1515.

**Park Royal Hotel**—This cozy inn on the north side of Vancouver's harbor has 30 nicely furnished rooms. This ivy-covered Tudor hotel has a lively English pub downstairs and extensive grounds on the Capilano River. Expensive. 540 Clyde Avenue, West Vancouver, BC V7T 2J7. 604/926–5511.

**West End Guest House**—This elegant pink Victorian offers seven guest rooms that are small but beautifully decorated with brass beds and antiques. The B&B is located between Stanley Park and the downtown shopping district. This is a non-smoking B&B. Moderate. 1362 Haro Street, Vancouver, BC V6E 1G2. 604/681–2889.

**Wedgewood Hotel**—This small, elegant inn offers European style, and 60 rooms and 33 suites, all magnificently furnished. This is an exceptional and classy hotel. Facilities include use of health club and pool. Expensive. 845 Hornby Street, Vancouver, BC V6Z 1V1. 604/689–7777, 800/663–0666.

## *Fine Dining in Vancouver:*

**Angelica**—This sophisticated restaurant always serves innovative and challenging dishes featuring local seafood and game. Moderate. 2611 W Fourth Avenue. 604/737–2611.

**Bishop's**—Owner John Bishop describes his cuisine as "contemporary home cooking." Well, dining at home was never like this. Bishop has created an innovative menu featuring touches of Pacific Rim, Northwest, French, and American nouvelle. The dishes are always colorful and a blend of subtle flavors. The menu isn't surprising—basic meats and local seafood—but the presentation and the creative pastas make this a special place. Expensive. 2183 W Fourth Avenue. 604/738–2025.

**Caffe de Medici**—Elegant northern Italian cuisine served in an intimate and beautiful room. Moderate. 1025 Robson Street. 604/669–9322.

**Corse Trattoria**—Mediterannean style and Italian cuisine, featuring the fresh of the Northwestern seafood. The result is a menu offering more than 50 pasta choices, the real gems here, and some surprisingly creative veal and seafood dishes. Moderate. 1 Lonnsdale. 604/987–9910.

**Le Crocodile**—The best country French cooking in Vancouver is found in this busy bistro just off Robson Street. Moderate. 818 Thurlow Street. 604/669–4298.

**Le Gavroche**—Located in an old house, this excellent French restaurant features some fine seafood and game dishes. The best choices, though, are the daily specials. Expensive. 1616 Alberni Street. 604/685–3924.

**Gerard's**—Excellent haute French cuisine served in an elegant, antique-furnished dining room at the Le Meridien Hotel. Expensive. 845 Burrard Street. 604/682–5511.

**Imperial**—The setting is magnificent: a renovated waterfront building with a high-ceilinged dining room decorated with an art deco flair. The cuisine is Cantonese seafood, and the dishes, particularly the fresh crab and lobster, are sensational. Moderate. In the Marine Building, 355 Burrard Street. 604/688–8191.

**Kirin Mandarin**—Often sensational Shanghai, Szechwan, and Beijing fare is served in this luxurious postmodern dining room. Moderate. 1166 Alberni. 604/682–8833.

**Monterey Grill**—Excellent Northwest cuisine, featuring seafood and local game. Moderate. In the Pacific Palisades Hotel, 1277 Robson Street. 604/688–0461.

**Umberto's Fish House**—An Italian seafood restaurant with a pleasant Mediterranean decor, flowers on the tables, and other nice touches. Try the ciopinno and the Dungeness crab dish with nutmeg, spinach, and bechamel sauce. Expensive. 1376 Hornby Street. 604/687–6621.

**The William Tell**—This dining room in the Georgian Court Hotel offers excellent Swiss-Continental cuisine, featuring fresh seafood and excellent game dishes. The three dining rooms are beautiful and elegant. Moderate/expensive. 765 Beattie Street (in the Georgian Court Hotel). 604/688–3504.

# Nightlife

These four cities offer a wide variety of nightlife. Here's a sampling of the best each has to offer:

# Edmonton:

The theatrical center of Edmonton is the four-stage Citadel Theatre Complex, considered by many to be the largest and most prolific theater in Canada. A wide variety of dramatic productions and musicals are offered there year-round. Call for the current schedule. (9828 101A Avenue; 403/425–1820).

The Edmonton Ballet Company (403/438–4350), the Edmonton Opera (403/482–7030), and the Edmonton Symphony Orchestra (403/428–1414) perform in the Jubilee Auditorium on the University of Alberta campus, 1415 114 Street.

For nightlife, consider The Sidetrack Cafe (10333 112 Street; 403/421–1326) for top music groups and comedy. For the best in country and western music, visit the Cook County Saloon (8010 103 Street; 403/432–0177) or the Rodeo Club (in the Kingsway Inn, 10812 Kingsway Avenue; 403/479–4266).

## *Portland:*

For theatrical productions, call the Artists Repertory Theatre (1111 SW 10th Avenue; 503/242–2400), which produces works by new playwrights and old standards; the Columbia Theater Company (2021 SE Hawthorne Boulevard; 503/232–7005), which performs works by American playwrights; the Portland Center Stage Shakespeare Festival (1111 SW Broadway; 503/248–6309), which presents five classic and contemporary plays each season; and the Portland Area Theatre Alliance Hot Line (503/241–4903), which keeps tabs on what's on stage in town.

The Oregon Ballet Theatre (503/227–6867) and the Portland Opera (503/228–1353) hold their events at the Portland Civic Auditorium (222 SW Clay Street; 503/248–4496), which also books touring rock and country performers.

The Oregon Symphony (503/228–1353) performs at the Arlene Schnitzer Concert Hall in the Portland Center for the Performing Arts (SW Broadway and Main Street; 503/228–1353). The hall is also used by touring rock stars, visiting Broadway shows, and other events.

For nightclubs, the most romantic spot is the Key Largo Night Club at 31 NW First Avenue. It has a garden dining room, dance floor, and great Cajun food. Call 503/223–9919.

For blues, consider the Dandelion Club at 31 NW 23rd Place; 503/223-0099. For jazz, the Hobbit (4420 SE 39th Avenue; 503/771-0742) and the Brasserie Montmarte (626 SW Park Avenue; 503/224-5552) are the top clubs.

## Seattle:

The top stages in town are the Seattle Repertory Theater (Bagley Wright Theater at Seattle Center, 155 Mercer Street; 206/443-2222), which presents nine classics and new plays each season; the New City Arts Center (1634 11th Avenue; 206/323-6800), which produces experimental plays; the Fifth Avenue Musical Theatre Company (1308 Fifth Avenue; 206/625-1468), which does four lavish musicals each year; and the Group Theater (3940 Brooklyn Avenue NE; 206/543-4327), which presents socially significant works.

The Pacific Northwest Ballet (206/547-5920) presents more than 60 shows each year at the Opera House at the Seattle Center. The Civic Light Opera (206/363-2809) performs three or four different works each season, while the Seattle Opera (206/443-4711) has been acclaimed for its productions at the Opera House at the Seattle Center.

The Seattle Symphony (206/443-4747) plays at the Opera House at the Seattle Center and the Northwest Chamber Orchestra (206/343-0445) performs at a number of city stages.

For nightclubs, the Ballard Firehouse (5429 Russell Street; 206/784-3516) is nationally known for its blues. Dimitrout's Jazz Alley (2037 Sixth Avenue; 206/441-9729) is famous for its local and national jazz stars. In Pioneer Square, the New Orleans Creole Restaurant (114 First Avenue S; 206/622-2563) has good live jazz while the nearby OK Hotel (212 Alaskan Way; 206/621-7903) offers solid rock and new wave music.

## Vancouver:

The Vancouver Playhouse (Hamilton at Dunsmuir Streets; 604/872-6722) and the Arts Club Theatre (1585 Johnston Street on

Granville Island; 604/687–1644) present popular theatrical shows.

The Vancouver Symphony Orchestra (604/684–9100) and the CBC Orchestra (604/662–6000) play at the Orpheum Theatre at 601 Smithe Street. The Early Music Society (604/732–1610) presents interesting medieval and rennaisance concerts throughout the year at various locations.

The Vancouver Opera (604/682–2871) presents four operas each season at the Queen Elizabeth Theatre at 600 Hamilton Street. This theater is also the local stop for visiting ballet companies.

On the nightclub scene, the best jazz is found at the Grunt Gallery (209 E Sixth Avenue; 604/875–9516) and Carnegie's (1619 W Broadway; 604/733–4141). Great pianists and vocalists are found at the Monterey Lounge in the Pacific Palisades Hotel (1277 Robson Street; 604/688–0461).

The towering mountains of Denali National Park in Alaska.
*(National Park Service photograph by M. Woodbridge Williams)*

CHAPTER 4

# The High and
# the Mighty

*T*here are so many towering mountains in the Pacific Northwest—16 summits in Alaska alone top 14,000 feet—that it is hard to compile a short list of the most magnificent peaks. Accessibility is the key factor in making our list, so we have selected five mountains that showcase nature's splendor.

The five mountains are, from north to south: Mt. McKinley in Alaska, known to the Athabascan Indians as Denali—"the high one"; Mt. Rainier and Mount St. Helens in Washington, both volcanoes, one sleeping and the other known for its massive eruption in 1980; Mt. Hood, a recreation paradise; and Crater Lake, a magical, almost mystical mountaintop lake formed when an ancient volcano blew the top off a mountain.

All five mountains are very special destinations. On their slopes you will find abundant animal life, dramatic scenery, adventures, and an awe-inspiring sense of wonder.

## Mt. McKinley

Mt. McKinley, the tallest summit on the continent, dominates the enormous and wondrous Denali National Park and Preserve. The mountain is so massive that it has two peaks—South Peak, the highest, hits 20,320 feet while the North Peak, two miles away, is 19,470 feet high. This enormous mountain, often shrouded in clouds and topped by ice and snow, makes the nearby Mt. Foraker (17,400 feet) and Mt. Silverthrone (13,220 feet) look small by comparison.

Mt. McKinley is the centerpiece, the defining element of the massive 9,375-square-mile Denali National Park and Preserve, a natural stage showcasing many of the finest and rarest attractions in the continent. Here visitors can see the giant Muldrow Glacier, which flows from Mt. McKinley's twin peaks almost to the park road. Visitors can see caribou, golden eagles, Dall's sheep, grizzly bears, and other wildlife.

A visit to this popular, often-crowded park starts at the Visitor Access Center on Highway 3 on the northeastern corner of the park. The Denali Park Road runs about 90 miles west into the park, but private vehicles can drive only the first 14.8 miles. Drivers must stop at the Savage River Check Station and board free shuttle buses or tour buses to go farther into this wonderland.

The park is a busy place with a wide variety of activities. You can go white water rafting on the Nenana River, take a tundra wildlife tour, hike the many miles of trails, watch dogsled demonstrations, go mountain climbing, ski cross-country, or go on an overnight backpacking trip. The best time to visit is between late May to mid-September, when the park roads are completely open and the summer day runs 24 hours. July and August are the most crowded times, followed by June. For mountain climbers, the best months are May and June. When the snows come, only the first three miles to the park headquarters are kept open by snowplows, drastically limiting access to Denali.

Even in the summer, driving is restricted because of the crowds. Private vehicles cannot drive past the Savage River Check Station, at Milepost 12.8 on the park road. For most visitors, the free shuttle bus tours are the way to explore this vast natural preserve. The buses make the 85-mile trip from the Visitor Access Center at the park entrance to Wonder Lake, at road's end, and back in 11 hours. Along the way you will see many of the wild animals mentioned earlier. If you want to stop and take a hike, simply ask the driver to let you off (although there are some prohibited areas). You can always flag down the next bus coming along.

After you leave the Savage River checkpoint, the road crosses the Primrose Ridge and then enters a marshy area whose willow trees attract many moose. The road continues west, crossing another bridge and then cutting through the Igloo and Cathedral Mountains, the home of the white Dall sheep. One of the rarer animals in the park is the grizzly bear, and the best place to spot them is at Sable Pass, just west of the Igloo Mountains. Because the bears are ferocious and have been known to attack humans, this is one of the few areas that you will not be allowed to get off the bus.

Beyond the bear country, the Denali Park Road crosses more rivers, slowly ascending until it reaches the 3,980-foot-high Highway Pass, the highest point on the road. Beyond the pass is the Stony Hill Overlook, where, weather permitting, you should be able to spot mighty Mt. McKinley. The Stony Hill area is also a popular feeding ground for the park's herds of caribou.

At Milepost 66 is the Eielson Visitor Center, an oasis with a great view of the mountains, wildflowers, and begging ground squirrels. The center has information and exhibits on the park, and the rangers often conduct talks and other nature-oriented activities. Check the schedule at the center for the day's events.

West of the center is the nose of the muddy, gravel-covered Muldrow Glacier, which flows more than 30 miles from Mt. McKinley to this point. The nearby ponds are home to loons, beavers, waterfowl, and occasionally moose.

Wonder Lake is the western end of the road. The bus will stop before making the return trip. Take time to look south and you will see the "high one"—Mt. McKinley.

## Mt. Rainier

Just three hours' drive from Seattle, the tallest mountain in the Cascades is a landmark of snow and ice whose frigid summit serenely hides its violent past. The 14,410-foot-high Mt. Rainier is one of the world's largest volcanoes, and is considered dormant but not extinct even though it last erupted more than a century ago.

Mt. Rainer National Park is a 235,404-acre preserve that offers more than just fantastic views of this Cascade peak. Here you can find fields of wildflowers, watch (and listen) as the mountain's 26 glaciers creep down its slopes, hike through dense forests, or catch glimpses of deer, bears, and mountain goats.

The park is open daily, though only the Nisqually-Paradise Road (one of four entering the park) is kept open all year. The best time to visit is July and August, if you want to see the animals and wildflowers. Winter is a popular time for cross-country skiing and snowshoe treks. Park naturalists lead nature and history walks, and conduct programs and activities for adults and children year-round. Check the various visitors' centers for the daily schedule of events.

Start your visit by entering the park on its southwest corner at the Nisqually–Paradise entrance. The road enters through a dense forest of red cedar, western hemlock, and Douglas fir. Six miles inside the park is the Longmire Museum, where early explorer James Longmire built the park's first hotel around the mineral spring he discovered there in 1883. The museum has interesting exhibits on the park's flora and fauna and its early history. Here you can find the Hiker Information Center or take an easy stroll on the half-mile-long Trail of the Shadows.

Drive for six more miles beyond the museum and you come to Ricksecker Point, where you can look south to the Tatoosh Range, a rugged area of ancient lava flows. North of you is Mt. Rainier and the Nisqually Glacier, one of six glacial flows that start at the mountain's ice cap. The next stop on this road is 1.5 miles beyond the lookout. There you will find the Narada Falls, a lovely 168-foot cascade. A short hike will take you along a marked trail to a viewing area below the bridge.

The next stop is three miles beyond the waterfalls, and it is likely to be the most crowded—a place aptly named Paradise. This is where you will find the Henry M. Jackson Memorial Visitor Center and the Paradise Inn, a historic lodge built in 1917. It is also here that you will find grand views of the snow-capped Mt. Rainier as well as fields of wildflowers—as many as 40 different varieties—covering the mountain's rolling foothills. The sight is incredibly beautiful when these flowers are in bloom.

The next drive is a 50-mile route taking you from Paradise to Sunrise. Watch for the turnoff for Sunrise and Yakima just after you leave Paradise. The road takes you past the scenic Reflection Lakes and to the overlook at Stevens Canyon, named after a climber who was one of the first to conquer Rainier. The waterfalls plunging over the canyon's walls are beautiful. The Canyon Stroll walk is an easy half-mile hike that offers excellent views of the gorge.

Continue driving east for another 9.5 miles until you come to the Grove of the Patriarchs, an easy 1.3-mile trail that takes you to an island in the Ohanapecosh River covered with Douglas fir and red cedar trees, many of them 500 to 1,000 years old. After taking the hike, drive east again until you come to the lefthand turnoff for Sunrise on Highway 123. (Highway 123 is also the southeastern access road in and out of the park.) Ten miles farther north on Highway 123, make a left on Highway 410, and drive to the sharp hairpin left turn for the White River Entrance and the Sunrise Visitor Center. (Highway 410 exits the extreme northeastern corner of the park and continues northwest to near Tacoma.)

Two easy hiking trails begin at the Sunrise Visitor Center. The Emmons Vista Trail, a four-mile trek, leads to a grand view of the Emmons Glacier. The Sourdough Ridge Natural Trail, a 1.5-mile hike, gives you a closer look at the wildflowers of this subalpine meadow. A more difficult hike from the center, but one that brings you seemingly face to face with Mt. Rainier, is the Burroughs Mountain Trail, a seven-mile hike that takes you through the tundra. The return is by the Sunrise Rim Trail.

The fourth access point of the park is via Highway 165 on the extreme northwest corner. This road, called the Carbon River Entrance, draws fewer crowds because the road is unpaved and the sights are not as dramatic as those on the Nisqually–Paradise highway.

The top attraction on this route is the Carbon River Rain Forest Park, a self-guided half-mile walk among the huge Douglas fir, Sitka spruce, and red cedar. The moist climate in this section of the park has draped the trees in moss. A tougher climb, but one that gives you a close-up look at the Carbon Glacier, leaves from the parking area of the nearby Ipsut Creek Campground. The seven-mile round trip hike is fairly steep and challenging but the views of the dirt-stained glacier are worth the effort.

## Mount St. Helens

Once one of the most beautiful volcanic mountains in the Cascades, Mount St. Helens changed forever on May 18, 1980. After weeks of rumbling and seething, the mountain just 48 miles north of Vancouver, Washington, literally blew its top. On that day an enormous eruption destroyed the top 1,313 feet of the 9,677-foot-high mountain, killing 57 people and devastating more than 200 square miles of forest. The plume of smoke and ash shot more than 16 miles into the air, turning day into night, clogging the mighty Columbia River with mud, and covering three states to the east with dirt and grit.

Since that cataclysm, Mount St. Helens has slowly returned to normal. Lush forests once scattered like some many matchsticks are coming to life again. Wildlife that seemed to have been eliminated has returned to the slopes.

Mount St. Helens sleeps, rumbling occasionally in its slumber. A visit here gives a close look at the enormous forces of nature that helped shape this section of the world.

Before visiting the 110,000-acre National Volcanic Monument, stop by one of three Forest Service information centers. The centers are located at Pine Creek, 18.5 miles east of the town of Cougar on Forest Service Road 90 near the southeast corner of the park, at Iron Creek, seven miles south of Randle at Forest Service Roads 25 and 76, and at Ape Cave, on Forest Service Road 8303 in the southern area of the park. The centers provide information on roads, volcanic activity, and other attractions in the preserve.

Access is limited to this national monument. The paved roads from the information centers do not traverse the park, but a number of gravel Forest Service roads branch off these paved highways and enter the volcanic park. These roads are frequently closed by snow from late October to June.

The major point of interest is the National Volcanic Mountain Visitor Center, five miles east of I-5 exit 49 on Highway 504 at Silver Lake. The center has a walk-in model of the mountain, films, and other exhibits. A short trail outside the center leads to views of the lake and volcano.

Another sight reachable by car is the Ape Cave, a 12,810-foot tunnel of lava, thought to be the longest such tube in the western hemisphere. This tube, on Forest Service Road 8303 (also called Cougar Creek Road) one mile west of Forest Road 83, was formed by a lava flow about 2,000 years ago. Stop by the Ape Cave Information Station before attempting to enter the tube. You will need a flashlight (several are preferred), warm clothes, and sturdy shoes to explore this lava cave.

Other scenic drives include Forest Service Road 26, which takes you to the major devastation zone; and Forest Service Road 99, which leads off Highway 25 to Meta Lake and comes within five miles of the volcano. This lookout offers the best view of the trail of destruction.

The best access is by hiking trails, see information portals for details. Guided climbs to the summit are conducted by park rangers. The 10-hour trek is difficult and is not for the inexperienced climber and hiker. Reservations must be made for the climb through park headquarters (206/247–5800). Visitors wishing to climb on their own will need a permit from park headquarters.

## Mt. Hood

The highest summit in Oregon, the 11,239-foot snow-capped Mt. Hood is the star attraction in the 1.1-million acre Mt. Hood National Forest, which stretches south from the mighty Columbia River to the Mount Jefferson Wilderness.

Of the five mountains in this chapter, Mt. Hood is the most accessible. Many roads cross the forest and mountain, bringing explorers to a land of lush forests, hot springs, waterfalls, glaciers, 4,000 miles of streams, more than 100 campgrounds, 150 lakes, flower-filled meadows, and miles of hiking paths, as well as skiing and other winter sports.

Before exploring this wonderland stop by the Mt. Hood Ranger Station in the village of Welches, just off on Highway 26 west of the town of Zigzag. The rangers have maps, brochures, and other information about the attractions in the wilderness.

Recreation is the major attraction here. In the winter, skiers and other adventurers flock to several winter sports areas in the park. A popular destination in winter or any season is Timberline Lodge, six miles north of the alpine resort village called Government Camp on Highway 26.

The Timberline Lodge is a true gem, one that you shouldn't miss if you aren't staying or dining there. The lodge is a 1930s WPA project that has lodging, restaurants, and other facilities for visitors, as well as a fine museum exploring pioneer life, Indians, and animals and plants common to the Cascades. Arts and crafts made in Oregon are on display throughout the lodge.

Everything in the lodge—the furniture, lamps, murals, paintings, and stonework—has been made by hand by Oregon artists. After viewing these delights, cross the road to the Wy'East Day Lodge, which serves as a museum of contemporary Oregon crafts as well as a ski shop in winter.

Near the lodges is the Palmer Ski Lift, which carries skiers up to the snow fields at the 8,500-foot level, an altitude where skiers can play even on many summer days.

After the snows melt way, the lodges remain popular destinations; the trails out of this resort lead to meadows streaked with colorful wildflowers.

Mt. Hood is also popular with mountaineers; many start their climbs at the Timberline Lodge. Guides will take novices up the slope in late spring and early summer, but only experienced climbers are allowed on the mountain in the winter. These expeditions are for adventurous only! Most climbs start about midnight and last from 10 to 15 hours.

In the summer, hikers, anglers, hunters, horseback riders, and campers flock to the national forest. For hikers, the Mt. Hood wilderness is heaven. More than 1,200 miles of trails lead through the national forest. Rangers can offer suggestions and maps for a variety of half-day, day, and overnight trips. One of the more popular trails is the Timberline Trail, a 37.5 route around the north and western sides of Mt. Hood. The scenery is fantastic, but this trip is strictly for experienced hikers. The terrain is often difficult and the length alone excludes most novices.

Other popular hiking trails are in the Salmon Huckleberry Wilderness and the Badger Creek Wilderness. These wilderness areas offer hiking trails for all skill levels as well as numerous campgrounds for those seeking a stay in the wilds.

## Crater Lake

Picture a deep blue lake ringed by cliffs that tower as high as 2,000 feet above the lake's surface. This serene 6,176-foot mountain hides its violent past beneath this deep layer of dark blue. Sixty centuries ago, the summit of the mountain called Mazama by the local Indians exploded, expelling so much ash and debris that the summit of the mountain collapsed. Over the years snow and rain collected in the 1,900-foot-deep depression, forming one of the deepest lakes in the nation as well as one of the more pristine and scenic delights in the Pacific Northwest.

You can enter the park from the west or south by Highway 62 or from the north via Highway 138. These roads enter the 183,227-acre national park and pass by entrance stations where you can pick up maps and other information about the activities and attractions here.

From the south or west, Highway 62 enters the park and comes to the Anne Spring Entrance Station, where you can take the turnoff for Rim Drive. This secondary road leads first to the Godfrey Glen Trail, a popular one-mile nature hike, and then to the Park Headquarters at Steel Center and the Rim Village Visitor

Center. This road is usually open to the visitor center year-round except after major snows. The northern road, Highway 138, opens June 15 and remains open until the first snow.

The Rim Drive, the scenic route around the lake, is open from mid-July to mid-October. This 35-mile-long road circles Crater Lake, passing numerous overlooks and picnic areas.

Start your tour at the Rim Village. A grand view of the lake can be had at the Sinnott Memorial Overlook near the village. Before leaving the village to take the Rim Drive, rangers suggest setting your car's odometer at zero, for the many sights are marked by mileage.

The first major attraction on the Rim Drive as you head west from the Rim Village is Discovery Point (1.3 miles). A party of gold prospectors discovered the lake at this point in 1853. In the distance on the left is Hillman Peak, an ancient volcano named after one of the prospectors.

At Mile 4 stop for a view of Wizard Island, a 700-foot-high cinder cone that resembles a sorcerer's hat. For a better view, hike 0.8 miles up the steep trail to the fire tower on the summit called The Watchman, just south of the overlook. The views from this 8,025-foot lookout are fantastic.

Continue driving around the lake, but be certain to bear right when the road forks at Mile 6.1. The road that is straight ahead is Highway 138, the entry route from the north. At Mile 8.8 is Steel Bay, named after William Gladstone Steel, who successfully lobbied President Theodore Roosevelt to make the lake a national park in 1902.

At Mile 10.7 is the one-mile-long Cleetwood Trail, a steep path leading down to the lake and the Crater Lake Boat Tours that leave from Cleetwood Cove. The trips leave hourly between 9:00 AM and 3:00 PM daily from July to early September. The cruises last two hours and park naturalists describe the scenery and discuss its history. Before taking this trip, remember that the climb back is difficult. The trail is the only access to the boat cruise.

At Mile 14.8 is the Skell Head lookout. At Mile 17 is the Mt. Scott Trail, which many consider the most sensational trail

Crater Lake National Park has to offer. The trail starts from the lefthand side of Rim Drive at Mile 17 and goes 2.5 miles up to the park's highest point. At Mile 17.4, a short turnoff takes you to Cloudcap, the highest (8,070 feet) lookout on the Rim Drive. From it you can see the Phantom Ship, a badly weathered rock that stands 160 feet above the lake surface and looks much like a sailing ship. Another view of the ship can be had at Kerr Notch (Mile 23.2).

Not every wonder in this park is found in the lake. At Mile 31.2 is the stop for the Castle Crest Wildflower Trail, a half-mile path that goes through a cedar and fir forest before entering a meadow filled with flowers in July and August.

Beyond the trail, the Rim Drive brings you back to the park headquarters, where you can either exit the park or return to Rim Village.

## For More Information

### Denali National Park:

**Denali National Park and Preserve**—c/o Superintendent, P.O. Box 9, Denali NP, AK 99755. 907/683–2294.

### Mt. Rainier National Park:

**Mt. Rainier NP**—Tahoma Woods, Star Route, Ashford, WA 98304. 206/569–2211.

### Mount St. Helens National Volcanic Monument:

**Mount St. Helens Monument Headquarters**—3029 Spirit Lake Highway, Castle Rock, WA 98611. 206/274–6644.

### Mt. Hood National Forest:

**Mt. Hood National Forest**—Supervisor's office, 2955 NW Division Street, Information Section, Gresham, OR 97030. 503/666–0700.

## Crater Lake National Park:

**Crater Lake NP**—c/o Superintendent, P.O. Box 7, Crater Lake, OR 97604. 503/594–2211.

# Where and When

## Denali National Park:

This park and preserve is open year-round via Highway 3, but access on the park's interior roads is usually limited by snow except from early June to mid-September.

**Visitor Access Center**—open daily late May to early September. Eielson Visitor Center open daily early June to mid-September. Call 907/683–2686 for a recorded message on hours and activities.

**Alaska Railroad**—Service to Denali from Anchorage and Fairbanks year-round, with reduced schedules from fall through Spring. The rail station is at the entrance to Denali National Park. Contact Passenger Services, P.O. Box 107500-AK, Anchorage, AK 05510. 907/264–2494.

**Denali Air**—Sightseeing tours by airplane of Mt. McKinley and Denali Park during the summer. Denali Air, Box 82, Denali Park, AK 99755. 907/683–2261.

**Denali Dog Sled Tours**—Sled dog excursions in the park when there is sufficient snow. The tours are offered at the park. Denali Dog Tours, Box 30, Denali NP, AK 99755. 907/683–2264.

**Denali Raft Adventures**—Guided float and whitewater trips on the Nenana River, with closeup views of wildlife and the park scenery. Located seven miles south of the park entrance at Milepost 231 on Highway 3. Trips last two to four hours and depart several times a day. Denali Raft Adventures P.O. Box 595, Denali NP, AK 99755. 907/683–2234; in the winter, 907/337–9604.

**Tundra Wildlife Tours**—Trips depart from the Denali Park Station Hotel at 6:00 AM and 3:00 PM daily from mid-May to mid-September. Reservations advised. 907/683–2215.

## Mt. Rainier National Park:

**The Henry M. Jackson Visitor Center** at Paradise is open 9:00 AM to 7:00 PM daily mid-June to Labor Day; 9:00 AM to 6:00 PM daily mid-May to mid-June and after Labor Day through October. Open 10:00 AM to 5:00 PM on weekends only the rest of the year. Call 206/569–2211.

**Longmire Museum**—Open 9:00 AM to 5:30 PM daily June-September; 9:00 AM to 4:30 PM the rest of the year.

**Ohanapecosh Visitor Center**—Open 9:00 AM to 6:00 PM daily mid-June through September; 9:00 AM to 5:00 PM Memorial Day to mid-June and October 1 through late October.

**Sunrise Visitor Center**—Open 9:00 AM to 6:00 PM daily July to mid-September.

**Campgrounds**—All closed in the winter except Sunshine Point. Call the park for reservations. Stays limited to 14 days.

**Rainier Mountaineering**—Guided climbs of the mountain, with the two-day climb to the summit the most popular. Paradise, WA 98397. 206/569–2227 in the summer, 206/627–6242 in the winter.

## Mount St. Helens National Volcanic Monument:

**The Visitor Center on Highway 504** east of Castle Rock is open daily 9:00 AM to 6:00 PM from early April to mid-September; 9:00 AM to 5:00 PM daily the rest of the year. Closed Thanksgiving and Christmas. Call 206/274–6644 for information, 206/274–4038 for recorded messages.

**Pine Creek, Iron Creek and Ape Cave Centers** open daily 9:00 AM to 6:00 PM in the summer, and early autumn depending on snow.

**Summit Climbs**—Call 206/247–5800 for information.

## Mt. Hood National Forest:

**Timberline Mountain Guides**—Timberline Lodge. Guided climbs of the mountain throughout the year. 503/548–1888.

**Ski resorts**—Contact the forest rangers or the Mt. Hood Recreation Association, 65000 E. Highway 26, Welches, OR

97067. Call 503/622–3162 for detailed information on ski slopes, lift tickets, and lodging.

### Crater Lake National Park:

**Crater Lake Boat Tours**—Departures from Cleetwood Cove from late June to early September. 503/594–2211.

**Rim Village Visitor Center**—Open 9:00 AM to 6:00 PM daily from early June through September.

**Steel Center**—Park headquarters. Open 9:00 AM to 6:00 PM daily except Christmas. 503/594–2211.

## Romantic Retreats

The romance found in these five very special mountains and parks is not in the accommodations or the restaurants you find there. The romance is in the unmatched beauty of the scenery, the exciting scenes of wildlife, and the never-ending surprises you will see along your journeys here.

These national parks offer limited accommodations that range from primitive campgrounds to standard (but not necessarily romantic) hotels and lodges. We list the in-park accommodations, because they are so convenient, as well as some superb inns and restaurants within 60 miles of a park entrance.

Here are our favorite places to stay and dine. But first, an explanation of our cost categories:

One night in a hotel, resort, or inn for two:

*Inexpensive*—Less than $75.
*Moderate*—$75 to $125.
*Expensive*—More than $125.

For dinner for two (wine and drinks not included):

*Inexpensive*—Less than $25.
*Moderate*—$25 to $50.
*Expensive*—More than $50.

## Denali National Park: Romantic Lodging

**Camp Denali and North Face Lodge**—There are 18 rustic cabins that share central showers at Camp Denali, and 15 rooms with showers at the North Face Lodge, three miles from Wonder Lake at Camp Denali. Expensive, two meals included. P.O. Box 67, Denali, NP, AK 99775. 907/683–2290 in the summer, P.O. Box 216 Cornish, NH 03746 and 603/675–2248 in the winter.

**Denali Mountain Lodge**—This modern 200-room motel is near Kantishan at the western end of the park road. Expensive, two meals are included. P.O. Box 229, Denali NP, AK 99755. 907/683–2643.

**Denali National Park Hotel**—The 100 rooms in this hotel are simply furnished and adequate for a short stay. The hotel is in the park and offers a shuttle bus to the most popular sights. The inn is open from mid May to early September. Expensive. 825 W Eighth Avenue, Suite 220, P.O. Box 87, Anchorage, AK 99501. 907/276–7234 in Anchorage, 907/683–2215 in Denali.

**Harper Lodge Princess**—Nicer than the Denali National Park Hotel, this 192-room motel, a half-mile from the entrance, is attractively decorated with Alaskan art. The rooms are pleasant and comfortable, and the views of the Nenana River are excellent. Open from late May to mid-September. Expensive. P.O. Box 110, Denali NP, AK 99755. 907/683–2282.

**McKinley Chalet Resort**—The finest lodging near the park is found at this 254-room cottage resort located one mile from the main entrance. The comfortable and attractive rooms are in two-story buildings located on a hillside, offering grand views of the mountains. Facilities include an indoor pool, sauna, and whirlpool. Open mid-May to late September. Expensive. 825 W Eighth Avenue, Suite 240, Anchorage, AK 99501. 907/276–7234 in Anchorage, 907/683–2215 in Denali.

## Denali National Park: Fine Dining

**Chalet Dining Room**—This fine restaurant in the McKinley Chalet Resort offers creative Northwest cuisine, featuring the best fish and fowl of Alaska. Open mid-May to late September. Moderate. Call for reservations. 907/683–2215.

## Mt. Rainier and Vicinity: Romantic Lodging

**Alexander's Country Inn**—Once a luxury hotel, this inn near the Nisqually entrance to the park faded over the years since it opened in 1912 as the Mesler Inn. It attracted such notables as Presidents Theodore Roosevelt and William Howard Taft. New owners have restored the inn and brought its 12 rooms back to the grandeur of other days. The inn is famous as a landmark because of its waterwheel and octagonal tower. The tower is where you will climb a narrow staircase to reach the Tower Suite, an antique and wicker-filled retreat. The hot tub, used by all guests, is a flight below. The 11 other rooms are furnished with antiques, country quilts, and other nice touches. The restaurant is a fine dining spot. Moderate. 37515 Star Route 706 E, Ashford, WA 98304. 206/569–2300, 800/654–7615.

**Ashford Mansion**—The spacious 1903 house offers four lovely guest rooms. Moderate. 30715 Mt. Tahoma Canyon Road, Box G, Ashford, WA 98304. 206/569–2739.

**National Park Inn**—This 25-room inn was built in 1926 and has recently been renovated. The rooms are pleasant but not outstanding. Seven rooms share baths. Moderate. Located six miles inside the park from the southwest entrance, at the 2,700-foot-level on Mt. Rainier. Mt. Rainier Guest Services, P.O. Box 108, Ashford, WA 98304. 206/569–2275.

**Old Mill House Bed and Breakfast**—This 1920s mansion, built by a local lumber baron, offers one outstanding suite and three pleasant rooms. The green, mauve, and gray Isadora Duncan suite includes a king-size bed, his and hers dressing rooms, private bath, and lots of charm. The inn is 24 miles west of the Nisqually entrance to the park. Moderate. P.O. Box 543, Eatonville, WA 98328. 206/832–6506.

**Paradise Inn**—Located at 5,400 feet inside the park near Mt. Rainier, this 126-room hotel offers stunning views of the mountains and glaciers. The rooms are pleasant but not exceptional. Moderate. The inn and restaurant are 20 miles east of the Nisqually entrance. Mt. Rainier Guest Services, Box 108, Ashford, WA 98304. 206/569–2275.

## Mt. Rainier and Vicinity: Fine Dining

**Alexander's Country Inn**—This elegant restored hotel has a fine restaurant featuring fresh trout and pasta dishes. Don't miss the berry pies. Moderate. Four miles east of Ashford on Highway 706. 206/569–2300.

**Paradise Inn**—The dining room at this hotel inside the park offers a standard American menu, heavy on the beef and seafood. The food is good, but not outstanding. Moderate. The inn and restaurant are 20 miles east of the Nisqually entrance. 206/569–2400.

**Wild Berry**—Located about a mile from the Nisqually entrance to Mt. Rainier Park, this attractive and bustling restaurant features excellent, but not gourmet, food. The staples here are pizzas, giant sandwiches, crepes, and mountain trout. Inexpensive. 37720 Highway 706 E, Ashford. 206/569–2628.

## Mount St. Helens and Vicinity: Romantic Lodging

**Red Lion Inn**—Located about 35 miles west of Mount St. Helens in the town of Kelso, this standard motel offers 163 unexciting but acceptable rooms. Moderate. 510 Kelso Drive (exit 39 on I-5), Kelso, WA 98626. 206/636–4400.

**Seasons Motel**—Located in Morton just north of the national monument, this 49-unit motel is closer than the Red Lion Inn and is just as good. Inexpensive. Located one block northwest of Highways 12 and 7. 200 Westlake, Morton, WA 98356. 206/496–6835.

## Mount St. Helens and Vicinity: Fine Dining

**Henri's**—This attractive restaurant serves fine American fare. Moderate. 4545 Ocean Beach Highway, Longview. 206/425–7970.

**Monticello Restaurant**—Seafood and Mexican cuisine are the featured dishes at this casual downtown Longview restaurant. Moderate. 1405 17th Avenue, Longview. 206/425–9900.

## *Mt. Hood and Vicinity: Romantic Lodging*

**Inn at Cooper Spur**—This inn between Mt. Hood and the town of Hood River offers six standard motel rooms and eight cozy cabins. Each cabin has two bedrooms, a sleep loft, a full kitchen, 1 1/2 baths, and a huge fireplace. Don't worry about cutting the wood—it's outside the door, near your own hot tub. Expensive. 10755 Cooper Spur Road, Mt. Hood, OR 97041. 503/352–6692.

**Mt. Hood Valu Inn**—This new motel is in the national forest, facing the ski areas. The rooms are spacious and attractive. Moderate. 87450 Government Camp Loop, Mt. Hood, OR 97028. 503/272–3205.

**Resort at the Mountain**—This lavish 200-room resort offers excellent, modern rooms, two and three-bedroom condos, indoor and outdoor pools, 27 holes of golf, six tennis courts, and other attractions. Expensive. 68010 E Fairway Avenue, Welches, OR 97067. 503/622–3101, 800/547–8054 outside Oregon, 800/452–4612 inside Oregon.

**Timberline Lodge**—We highly recommend this wonderul lodge. It is a 1937 WPA project, and is a marvel in carved wood and stone. There are 59 rooms with fireplaces. The rooms are comfortable and pleasant. Facilities include a ski lift, heated pool, sauna, and award-winning restaurant. Expensive. Timberline, OR 97028. 503/272–3311, 800/547–1406.

## *Mt. Hood and Vicinity: Fine Dining*

**Cascade Dining Room**—This dining room in the magnificent Timberline Lodge features excellent fresh seafood and pasta dishes. Moderate. Timberline. 503/272–3311.

**Chalet Swiss**—Fondues, sautees, and fresh seafood are served in this country-Swiss dining room. Moderate. Highway 26 at Welches Road, Welches. 503/622–3600.

**Highland Dining Room**—The restaurant at the Resort at The Mountain features fine game and seafood dishes. Moderate. 68010 E Fairway Avenue, Welches. 503/622–3101.

**Inn at Cooper Spur**—Good, but not exceptional American fare at this inn's dining room. Moderate. 10755 Cooper Spur Road, Mt. Hood. 503/352–6037.

## *Crater Lake and Vicinity: Romantic Lodging*

**Mazama Village**—There are 40 two-bedroom cabins at this resort, the only one in the park. Moderate. P.O. Box 128, Crater Lake, OR 97604. 503/594–2511.

**Thompson's Bed and Breakfast by the Lake**—Located about 48 miles south of the park in Klamath Falls, this B&B offers three pleasant guest rooms with spectacular views of Upper Klamath Lake, visiting deer, and the Cascades. Inexpensive. 11420 Wild Plum Court, Klamath Falls, OR 97601. 503/882–7938.

## *Crater Lake and Vicinity: Dining*

**Mazama Village**—This dining room at this lodge is the only restaurant in the park besides the one at Rim Village Visitor Center. Inexpensive. 503/594–2511.

The Blue Glacier on Mt. Olympus in Olympic National Park.
*(National Park Service photograph)*

CHAPTER 5

# Scenic Tours

*T*he Pacific Northwest is filled with dramatic scenery. Yet even within this wonderland of visual delights there are some special regions where the scenery is so stunning that a tour is a must.

These regions are the lush, mountain-topped Olympic Peninsula, the stunningly rugged Oregon Coast, the Oregon Trail region where the Old West still reigns, and the dramatic highways in the Washington Cascades. These four trips are designed to be made by car. The fifth tour we outline is by a special train that carries you through some of the most fantastic mountain scenery on the continent.

Here's your itinerary:

## The Olympic Peninsula

This 85-mile by 75-mile peninsula in the northwest corner of Washington is wild, wonderful, and delightfully contradictory. Here you can find rain forests as well as farmland dry enough to require irrigation, subtropical vegetation as well as ancient glaciers, storm-ravaged shores and beaches washed by a gentle inland sea, quaint Victorian towns and rustic mountain cabins and lodges.

The peninsula is reachable by ferry or by road, if you approach it via I-5 and Highway 101. Highway 101 is the busiest route, but gives you a close look at the majesty of the Olympic Mountains as you drive north to Port Townsend. Another approach, with charming villages and water views, is by the Kitsap Peninsula, a region east of the Olympic Peninsula bordered by the Hood Canal on the west and Puget Sound on the east. The Kitsap Peninsula is one of two small peninsulas (the other is the Long Beach Peninsula in southwestern Washington) that border the majestic Olympic Peninsula.

You can drive through the Kitsap Peninsula on your way to the Olympic Peninsula by taking Highway 16 north from Tacoma. This route takes you through Gig Harbor, a fishing community with some nice antique shops; Port Orchard, whose grand Olde Central Antique Mall graces Bay Street; and Poulsbo, an enclave of Norwegians whose heritage is reflected in its festivals and shops. Another way is to take the ferry from Seattle to Winslow on Bainbridge Island and browse through the art galleries and gift shops on Winslow Way before going on north. You can also reach the Olympic Peninsula by taking the ferry from Keystone on Whidbey Island to Port Townsend, a delightful Victorian fishing village described in Chapter 1; where this 216-mile tour of the Olympic Peninsula starts.

From Port Townsend drive south on Highway 20 until you come to Highway 101. Then turn west and drive ten miles to the charming farming town of Sequim, near the mouth of the Dungeness River. Sequim is a colorful waterfront community, known for its lighthouse as well as the Dungeness National Wildlife Refuge, which is home to thousands of migratory waterfowl and seals. The Dungeness Spit, part of the refuge, is a sandy beach area famed for its clams—you may want to stop and dig for a few. In town, the Sequim Natural History Museum explores the peninsula's bird and wildlife population, while the Sequim-Dungeness Museum has remains of 12,000-year-old mastadons and other Ice Age creatures, as well as exhibits on Indians and the first colonists. The Cedarbrook Herb Farm at 986 Sequim Avenue S sells a variety of herbs, unusual vegetables, and plants.

Seven miles west of Sequim on Highway 101 is Port Angeles, another Victorian town and fishing port that is the stop for the ferries to Victoria, B.C., due north across the Strait of Juan de Fuca. Port Angeles is also the gateway to the 1,441-square mile Olympic National Park and the Olympic National Forest.

Olympic National Park is one of the nation's unsung treasures, a wonderland of glacier-topped mountains, meadows filled with gaily colored flowers, deep ravines that howl with the wind, and rain forests that nurture myriad forms of life.

Before starting your trip, stop by the park headquarters at 600 E Park Avenue in Port Angeles for a weather report, maps, and other helpful information. The weather report is necessary because the main road into the park—Hurricane Ridge Road—takes you into the region named after the fierce winds that can strike without much warning in the winter months.

From Port Angeles you take the Hurricane Ridge Road into the national park. The change in scenery from the gentle beaches at Port Angeles is very dramatic on this road, which twists and turns as it climbs. The driving is safe and well worth the time. When you reach the Hurricane Ridge, stop for a moment next to the sign that serves as a locator for the major Olympic Mountains. From this point you can see Mt. Olympus, a true citadel of the gods, and several of its seven glaciers. Mt. Olympus's Blue Glacier gets an estimated 500 inches of snow a year, and is just one of more than 60 glaciers in this icy wonderland.

A mile farther along the road is the visitors lodge, where you can stop and walk along a nature trail into the Hurricane Hills, where the views are sensational.

The road continues another eight miles, become more and more rocky along the way. For the adventurous, the drive is well worth the effort—at road's end is Obstruction Peak, the finest view of the 7,965-foot-high Mt. Olympus and its sister peaks in the park.

The glaciers you see are remnants of the Ice Age, the climatological event that shaped the peninsula and the coast here, and also had the serendipitous effect of creating 16 species of flowers and animals seen nowhere else on earth. These include the Mazama pocket gopher, the Beardslee trout, the Olympic magenta painted cup, and the Olympic marmot.

After visiting this region of the park, return to Highway 101. The Hurricane Ridge Road is one of a dozen spur roads that lead off Highway 101 into the park, but do not traverse it. Each road leads to various hiking trails, camping areas, and park visitor centers.

Back downhill in Port Angeles, two attractions are worthy of your attention. The Arthur D. Feiro Aquarium has exhibits on the local sea life and the Clallam County Historical Museum has collections on the lives of Indians and colonists who lived on the peninsula.

West of Port Angeles, the road divides, with Highway 112 continuing west to the extreme northwest tip of the peninsula. This road takes you past small towns that cater to salmon fisherman. Continue west on Highway 101 to another scenic delight, the beautiful Lake Crescent, a postcard-like setting popular with campers and anglers. At the western end of the lake is Soleduck Road, which leads to Sol Duc Hot Springs, three thermal pools that you can bathe in. The temperature of the pools is 98 to 104 degrees, and they attract crowds of bathers in the summer.

Continue on Highway 101 until you come to the logging town of Forks and the turnoff for La Push, a scenic oceanfront village and the tribal headquarters of the Quillayute Indians. Take time to walk the trails to the excellent beaches, where the scenery can be quite dramatic.

The next turnoff south of Forks on Highway 101 is Hoh Road. This leads into the Hoh Rain Forest, an area that gets more than 140 inches of rain a year—a figure that makes Seattle's 36 inches a year seem like a mere passing mist.

The rain forest is a lush wonderland of nature, home to a suprising variety of animals and vegetation. The Hoh Visitor Center at road's end has exhibits, nature trails, and a museum. The rangers there lead hikes into the forest and can answer any questions you have.

From this point you can return to Highway 101 and either drive south to Aberdeen and then east on Highway 8 and I-5 to Olympia, Tacoma, and Seattle, or you can continue past Aberdeen on Highway 101 for 60 miles to the Long Beach Peninsula on the southwestern Washington coast.

This small finger of land is just north of the mouth of the mighty Columbia River, and offers 28 miles of sandy beaches, marshes filled with a wide variety of waterfowl and birds, and a quaint village or two.

Highway 101 takes you to Seaview, which is at the southern end of the Long Beach Peninsula. From this seaport you can turn south for Fort Canby State Park, a popular place for fishermen and bird-watchers. The Lewis & Clark Interpretive Center examines the 8,000-mile exploration of those two explorers. North of Seaview are such fishing villages as Nahcotta, Ocean Park, and Oysterville and, at the extreme northern tip, Leadbetter State Park, another wildlife refuge and bird-watching haven.

## *The Oregon Coast*

This 339-mile-long stretch of coast is a journey filled with breathtaking scenery and delightful port towns. Start the trip in Astoria, at the meeting of the majestic Columbia River with the Pacific Ocean, where Meriwether Lewis and William Clark began their fur trading enterprise with the assistance of John Jacob Astor.

Astor's name was given to the small village when it was founded in 1811. It is a busy port town with some nice B&Bs, a few interesting museums, and historic sites.

The Columbia River Maritime Museum has excellent maritime exhibits, including many personal belongings from the crews on the more than 2,000 ships lost in the treacherous waters where the river meets the sea. The museum is on 17th Street near Marine Drive.

You can take a closer look at the lifestyle of nineteenth-century mariners at the Flavel House/Heritage Museum, a Queen Anne Victorian at 441 Eighth Street. It was built in 1883 by Captain George Flavel, a wealthy shipping baron, and displays furnishings from that era, many of which were acquired by Flavel.

These mariners came after Lewis and Clark, whose explorations of the region in the early 1800s are celebrated at the Ft. Clatsop National Memorial, on Highway 101 six miles south of Astoria. A replica of the explorers' log stockade is at the park, and costumed rangers recreate the lifestyle of the times, doing some of the daily chores Lewis and Clark must have undertaken.

Ten miles south of this historic site is Seaside, an ocean resort town that enjoyed a rebirth in the 1980s after it spruced up its downtown. Seaside's main street is the Prom, a two-mile-long concrete boardwalk that attracts large crowds in the summer.

South of Seaside, the coast scenery grows more dramatic. Ecola State Park, Indian Beach, and Tillamook Head, all about nine miles south of Seaside, have some fantastic rocks expertly carved by sea and wind. A mile further is Cannon Beach, an upscale resort town that attracts a better-heeled crowd than Seaside and is famous for its sandcastle contest, held every May. Hemlock Street, the main thoroughfare, is lined with art galleries (don't miss the arts and crafts at White Bird or the photographs at the Haystack Gallery), restaurants, and boutiques.

Shopping, though, isn't the focus of attention here. On the wide beach is the 235-foot-high Haystack Rock, a mighty monolith popular with photographers. The sides of the rock are very slippery, and shouldn't be climbed.

The coastal delights continue past Haystack Rock. Oswald West State Park has a spectacular beach with tidal pools. The next town, Tillamook, is a dairy and fishing community whose Blue Heron French Cheese Factory on Highway 101 is a great place to sample cheese and local wines.

Tillamook's other attractions include the fascinating natural history displays at the Pioneer Museum, located in the 1905 Courthouse, and the beautiful scenery found along Three Capes Loop, a drive you reach by taking Third Street west in Tillamook. The drive takes you past the Cape Meares State Park and its century-old lighthouse and sea lions; Cape Lookout, where the coastal views can be excellent; and Cape Kiwanda, a hang gliding haven.

Back on Highway 101, continue south, bypassing Lincoln City (a town we feel is too commercial to enjoy), and come instead to Cape Foulweather, whose pines have been bent by the fierce winds that often blow here.

The next stop is the charming village of Newport, which has a nice waterfront and some interesting shops and galleries. The Wood Gallery at 818 SW Bay Boulevard features fine sculpture, woodwork, and pottery.

For a close up look at the area's marine life, visit the Undersea Gardens at 250 SW Bay Boulevard and the Hatfield Marine Science Center at 2030 Marine Science Drive.

After Newport comes a bit of whimsy. In the town of Seal Rock, on Highway 101, is the attraction called Seal Gulch, a life-sized ghost town whose inhabitants were carved with a chain saw by Ray Kowalski. It's an interesting place and well worth a visit.

The next village is Yachats, a small village with some nice restaurants and B&Bs and lovely, empty beaches. The natural wonders continue south of town. First is Cape Perpetua, a bluff with grand views of the sea below. Then, in order, Heceta Head and its magnificent lighthouse, Devil's Elbow State Park, and the Darlingtona Botanical Wayside—all excellent places to stop if you want to commune with nature.

The next town on the tour is Florence, a picturesque port city with some fine shops and restaurants, and the Oregon Dunes National Recreation Area—the 41-mile-long gem of the southern Oregon coast.

In this 32,000-acre recreation area you can find sand dunes more than 300 feet high, fishing piers, an old lighthouse, and other attractions. Stop by the park headquarters at 84505 Highway 101 in Florence to get maps and materials on the area's attractions.

South of the Dunes Area is Coos Bay, a town whose name is far more inviting than the reality of its industrial port atmosphere. Coos Bay is trying to repair its image, though, and is remodeling the waterfront area and the downtown mall.

Beyond Coos Bay is North Bend, the gateway to the Golden and Silver Falls State Park, where you can see two beautiful waterfalls more than 200 feet high.

Next is Charleston, a small town whose main attractions are the more than 300 species of birds at the South Slough National Estuarine Reserve and the splendid English and Japanese gardens at Shore Acres Botanical Gardens.

Continue south, bypassing the towns and parks as you aim toward Port Orford and the stretch of Highway 101 between that

♣

# UNDERGROUND WONDERLAND

The Oregon Caves, located 20 miles east of Cave Junction on Highway 46, are vast underground caverns first discovered in 1874 by Elijad Davidson, an early settler who was hunting deer in the area. In 1909, President Taft declared the caves a national monument, moved perhaps by poet Joaquin Miller's 1907 praise of the caverns as the "Marble Halls of Oregon."

The Oregon Caves are magnificent. You can join a guided tour and walk through chambers and corridors, passing by places called the Ghost Chamber, Neptune's Grotto, King's Plaza, and Paradise Lost. The tours are offered from 9:00 AM to 5:00 PM May through September, with longer hours in the summer. In the winter months, tours are offered at 10:30 AM, 12:30 PM, 2:00 PM and 3:30 PM. Visitors can stay in the rustic Caves Chateau, a 22-room lodge set in a forested canyon near the caves. Call 503/592–3400. Rates are moderate.

The caves are on Highway 26, about 20 miles east of Cave Junction in southern Oregon. Call 503/592–3400 for information about the caves.

town and Brookings. Highway 101 is hundreds of feet above the sea in this stretch, offering some of the finest views of the ocean and shore in Oregon. The scenery can be breathtaking, all the more reason to stop at the many overlooks.

In between Port Orford and Brookings is Gold Beach, where the magnificent Rogue River meets the sea. The town is a center of outfitters offering jet boat trips up the Rogue.

By the time you come to the fishing center of Brookings, you know you will have seen the best the Oregon coast has to offer.

## *The Oregon Trail and the Old West*

Parallel grooves stretch for miles in the hills and valleys of northeast and central Oregon. The ruts, carved by the wheels of heavily loaded wagons, are the remnants of the Oregon Trail, the legendary trek from Independence, Missouri, to the Oregon Territory. An estimated 350,000 emigrants made the difficult journey between 1841 and the 1890s.

The Oregon Trail almost parallels I-84, the superhighway that takes months off the journey these hardy pioneers struggled to complete. Rest areas along I-84 in this section of the state offer displays and exhibits on the pioneers and their experiences along the trail.

This pioneer heritage remains alive in the towns and countryside of eastern Oregon. This is where the Old West is remembered and relived every day.

Start a tour of this region in Pendleton, the center of the state's wheat-farming district. Pendleton is a western town, one where big hats and cowboy boots are as common as pickup trucks and horses. The major attraction in town is Hamley's Western Store at 30 SE Court. Hamley, a saddle maker since 1905, has displays on the saddles and a small gallery of western art.

Every September, Pendleton holds its Round-Up, a major rodeo that attracts thousands of visitors. The weeklong event includes the Happy Canyon Pageant, a tepee encampment of Northwest Indian tribes, and dancing and ceremonial activities. The major event of the Round-Up is the Westward Ho parade with costumed characters depicting pioneers.

The rodeo is celebrated at the Round-Up Hall of Fame, which honors the toughest cowboys and broncs (call for an appointment). Native American culture is honored at the Vert Museum, which has a fine collection of Indian artifacts and art.

From Pendleton, drive east on I-84 to La Grande and make the turn north on Highway 82 to Elgin, the headquarters of rafting outfitters, for trips down the Grande and Minam rivers, and, 51 miles further, the small town of Joseph.

Joseph is the gateway to the Wallowa Valley, a rugged landscape of canyons and rivers. The Nez Pierce Indians once lived here and called it "the valley of the winding rivers." An 1855 treaty granted the land to the tribe, but it was broken in 1875 when President Grant opened the region to settlers. In 1877, the Nez Pierce were ordered off the land and told to move to a new reservation. The forced move was fought unsuccessfully by the Indians, led by Young Chief Joseph.

The town of Joseph was named to honor that leader. Nez Pierce artifacts can be seen at the Wallowa County Museum, which is located in a renovated 1888 bank that was the site of a famous robbery.

From Joseph you can take a sidetrip by returning to Enterprise, six miles back west on Highway 82, and driving north for about 50 miles on Highway 3 to Flora. This once-thriving community is now a ghost town, filled with weathered, empty buildings slowly being invaded by wildflowers.

Joseph is also the gateway to other attractions. Take Forest Service Road 39 to Imnaha and the 603,150-acre Hells Canyon National Recreation Area. A steep gravel road leads from Imnaha up Grizzly Ridge to the Hat Point lookout, where more than a mile below you can see the Snake River. Other roads lead south from the Joseph–Imnaha road into the recreation area. Hells Canyon has a number of scenic delights and recreational opportunities. This is where you will find the nation's deepest canyon (7,993 feet, measured from He Devil Mountain to Granite Creek), the wild Snake River, and a landscape that varies from desert to snow-topped mountains. Hells Canyon is home to big horn sheep, mule deer, elk, cougar, and other wild animals. Outfitters offer float and jetboat trips down the Snake.

If the Hells Canyon drive is too far or too challenging, take the Forest Service Road 39 south from Joseph, which heads 40 miles to Highway 86. There you can turn north and drive to Homestead, a gold and silver mining town that has recently enjoyed a rebirth, and west to Halfway and the turnoffs for two ghost towns: first Cornucopia, which died in 1940 (the turnoff is in Halfway), and then Sparta, which disappeared after the Civil War (turnoff 12 miles farther west).

The next stop west on Highway 86 is Baker City, called the

# OREGON'S HOUSE OF MYSTERY

The Oregon Vortex is one of those natural wonders that defies explanation: this mysterious, invisible force changes perspective (your companion may look taller), makes it difficult to stand upright, allows balls to roll uphill and other feats that defy the laws of physics. The Vortex is located in the House of Mystery near Gold Hill, in southern Oregon. It's no trick. Physicist John Lister conducted hundreds of experiments to determine what was causing these bizarre acts and concluded that they were the result of an invisible, powerful whirlpool of energy. If you would like to try your own experiments, drive one mile west of Gold Hill on Highway 234 and follow the signs to the House. The House of Mystery's number is 503/855–1543.

Queen City of the Mines. This busy city has a lovely historic district that is so authentic-looking it was used as the set of the movie "Paint Your Wagon." The historic structures are in the 15-block area from the river to Fourth Street, bounded by Estes and Campbell streets.

More of the Old West can be seen at the Oregon Trail Regional Museum, 2490 Grove Street. It has artifacts from early pioneer life as well as an extensive collection of minerals, rocks, and semiprecious stones. The Eastern Oregon Museum, nine miles north on Highway 30, has more artifacts, toys, and relics from the early days.

Baker City is surrounded by some magnificent countryside. The Sumpter Valley Railroad, located 30 miles south on Highway 7, makes trips into a wildlife habitat and the mining district. The steam-driven locomotive pulls the passengers in two observation cars.

## *The Rocky Mountaineer*

Often called the "most spectacular train trip in the world," The Rocky Mountaineer journeys into some of the most incredible landscape the Pacific Northwest has to offer.

This modern, comfortable train makes a two-day, 600-mile journey between Vancouver and Calgary, retracing the route created by the 1856 Gold Rush.

The first stop is Kamloops, a town of 65,000 founded in 1812 as a fur trading outpost. Kamloops is in the semiarid desert region, an oddity in the often lush Northwest.

Passengers depart the train in Kamloops and spend the night in one of several hotels. The next morning, the train divides, with one train continuing on to Jasper and the other heading to Banff and Calgary.

Both of these second legs go through some of the finest scenery in Canada. The Canadian Rockies are stunning. Here you will see glaciers, mountains topping 10,000 feet, rushing rivers, alpine lakes, and meadows tinted with pastels.

The train to Jasper goes through the spectacular Yellowhead Pass, cutting through the Premier Mountain Range and passing the shore of exquisite Moose Lake.

The Banff–Calgary train crosses the majestic Continental Divide, the breathtaking Banff National Park and dramatic Kicking Horse Pass.

Both trips offer numerous opportunities to spot bear, moose, eagles, bighorn sheep and other wild animals who live in the wonderful countryside.

The Rocky Mountaineer trains run from May through October, depending on the weather. The passenger cars are luxurious, with reclining seats and large sightseeing windows. The trains travel in the daylight hours so passengers can see the beautiful scenery.

For a couple, the tours cost about $600 per person (U.S. dollars) roundtrip, or $350 one-way on the Vancouver to Jasper or Banff route; $675 roundtrip or $380 one-way on the Vancouver–Calgary run. The fare includes two breakfasts and two lunches (and one light dinner served to Calgary passengers east-bound from Banff), accommodations in Kamloops, and transfers to the hotel. Prices, of course, are subject to change.

## *The Washington Cascades*

Forged by fire and carved by ice, the Cascades form a great wall so impenetrable and so high that they divide Washington into two distinct climates—the wet west and the dry east.

This unbroken chain of mountain peaks and isolated volcanoes is a wonderland of striking scenery, wilderness areas, federal parklands, dramatic summits, and countless waterfalls—the natural wonders that gave the mountains their name.

Experiencing these wonders is easy, for three highways traverse the north and central Cascades, offering an often breathtaking passage into a realm whose king is an extinct volcano called Rainier. (Mt. Rainier and the other major peaks of the Cascades are discussed more fully in Chapter 4.)

The three Cascade highways are:

♠ Highway 20, the North Cascades Highway, a two-lane road connecting the Puget Sound with the mountains. This is the most scenic road, but a route usually closed by the snows from November to April.

♠ Highway 2, the Stevens Pass Highway, a two-lane (and occasionally four-lane) road from Everett across the mountains. This road is open year-round.

♠ I-90, the Snoqualmie Pass Highway, the fastest route east. Popular with truckers, I-90 is open year-round.

These roads can be combined with Highway 97 to form a loop from the Puget Sound area through the Cascades and back again. Along the way you will see some stunning scenery, visit parks and wilderness areas, and pass through some interesting mountain towns. Here's a guide for a drive into the Cascades.

**Highway 20**—The North Cascades Highway starts 70 miles north of Seattle and runs east from I-5 through the North Cascades National Park and the Ross Lake National Recreation Area before meeting Highway 97.

The drive east from the gentle farmlands of the Skagit River Valley is undramatic at first. It is only after you leave the lush farmlands that Highway 20 begins to climb, entering a thick forest and then passing a series of small towns in the Skagit River Valley, a region that draws hundreds of eagles in the winter. Concrete, the first town you come to, has a few shops and gas stations (the last you will see for awhile). Next is Rockport, about 115 miles east of Puget Sound, the gateway to the North Cascades National Park.

This park is often called the American Alps. Within its 684,000 acres are virgin forests, subalpine meadows, hundreds of glaciers, and a wide variety of animal life, including black bears, mountain goats, mule deer, and black-tailed deer. The park is popular with hikers, backpackers, and mountaineers.

After you drive east of Rockport you come to Marblemount and the park service headquarters, where you can pick up maps, brochures, and other information from the rangers there.

You enter the Ross Lake National Recreation Area 6.5 miles east of Marblemount. The drive here is easy, but the mountains just to the north bear names that offer silent testimony to the treachery and promise found in these slopes: Mt. Despair (7,293 feet), Mt. Terror (7,151 feet), Mt. Fury (8,291 feet), Mt. Prophet (7,579 feet), and Mt. Triumph (7,271 feet).

The Skagit River parallels the road in this section of the park. Farther up the road, the Seattle City Light's hydroelectric dams form Diablo and Ross Lakes. City Light offers an interesting four-hour Skagit Tour, which includes a boat cruise on the beautiful Diablo Lake and a ride up the mountain. You must sign up for these trips in Seattle at the City Light's main office at 1015 Third Avenue (206/684–3030).

The forest in this part of the Cascades is lush red cedar and hemlock, fed by the many streams and the ample rains. A close look at this forest can be had on the Thunder Woods Nature Trail, a one-mile loop that starts behind the amphitheater at the Colonial Creek Campground, about four miles beyond Diablo. The steep hiking trail goes through groves of cedar more than 300 years old.

At milepost 132 is the Diablo Lake Overlook, where you can see the 7,776-foot-high Colonial Peak and its glacier-carved sides. After this overlook, Highway 20 leaves the Cascades Park and enters the Okanogan National Forest and comes first to Rainy Pass, where you can see the striking differences between the wet, lush forests of the western slope and the arid, pine- and sage-brush-filled slopes of the eastern Cascades. The next major stop is the Washington Pass Overlook, which is at 5,438 feet above sea level and is the highest point of this highway.

Due south is Liberty Bell Mountain (7,808 feet), which is popular with climbers. Look closely and you might see some mountaineers. After this overlook the road begins to descend, heading southeast into the Methow Valley and a few towns. The one place to stop at is Winthrop, which fancies itself as the Old West, complete with wooden sidewalks, false-front stores, Old West festivals, and similar entertaining tourist attractions.

After a visit here, continue on Highway 20 until you come to Highway 97, which you take to bring you back to Highway 2 or I-90 to complete the Cascades loop.

**Highway 2**—The Stevens Pass Highway, as it is also known, runs east from Everett on the Sound, passing farmland, logging towns, and some quaint villages on its way into the rugged canyons of the Cascades.

The first stop on this highway is the town of Snohomish, a farming town just five miles east of Everett. Snohomish has renovated the Victorian buildings along its main street and filled them with restaurants and antique shops. Continue driving east to Wallace Falls State Park, where you can take a three-hour round-trip hike to a 265-foot waterfall.

Farther east, in the Snoqualmie National Forest, is Skykomish, an old logging town set in a rugged, mountainous setting.

# RESORTS WITH EVERYTHING

The Pacific Northwest has some excellent resorts that offer a wide range of activities. Here is our list of the best resorts:

**Banff Springs Hotel**—Picture a century-old Scottish castle perched in the mountains next to a lake and you have the wonderful Banff Springs Hotel. Antiques fill the 834-room hotel, which also offers lots of activities: 27 holes of golf, tennis, skiing, game room, exercise equipment, and more. This is a very special place, with an ambience that few modern luxury hotels can match. Expensive. Banff, AB, Box 960, T0L 0C0. 403/762–2211, 800/828–7447 (from the United States).

**Jasper Park Lodge**—Some of the views of Lac Beauvert and the Rockies from the rooms here are simply spectacular. The lodge has 416 modern and comfortable rooms, a heated pool, tennis courts, riding stables, an 18-hole golf course, exercise equipment, lawn games, nightclub, and other diversions. Expensive. Box 40, Jasper, AB T0E 1E0. 403/852–3301, 800/828–7447 (from the United States), 800/642–3817 (within Alberta), 800/268–9411 (rest of Canada).

**Kah-Nee-Ta Resort**—This interesting resort, built by the Confederated Tribes of Warm Springs Reservation, offers an 18-hole golf course, tennis, horseback riding, rafting on the Deschutes River, fishing, a mineral-spring pool, and mineral baths. The resort has 139 rooms in the arrowhead-shaped lodge, which is filled with Indian art. The rooms are small but comfortable—ask for the Chief Suite, the most spacious. More spacious accommodations can be found in tepees and cottages in the village a mile away, though there you have to bring a sleeping bag. The lodge restaurant features modified Native American dishes. Expensive. P.O. Box K, Warm Springs, OR 97761. 503/553–1112, 800/831–0100.

**108 Golf and Country Inn Resort**—An 18-hole golf course, five tennis courts, horseback riding, swimming pool, two lakes, and fantastic cross-country skiing in the winter on 200 kilometers of groomed trails make this resort a special place. There are 62 rooms, all recently remodeled and comfortable. Moderate. Box 2, RR1, 100 Mile House, BC V0K 2E0. 604/791–5211.

**Paradise Ranch Inn**—This inn lives up to its name combining the activities of a resort—swimming, fishing, bicycling, boating, tennis, and golf—with the atmosphere of a small inn. There are only 18 rooms, all spacious and furnished in Early American style, with the best overlooking the ponds. Expensive. 7000-D Monument Drive, Grants Pass, OR 97526. 503/479–4333.

**Salishan Lodge**—One of the most famous lodges in the Northwest, this magnificent, 200-room resort offers posh accommodations in eight-plex units located around the resort's 18-hole golf course. Rooms have fireplaces, balconies, local art, and great views of the grounds. You can golf, play tennis, go hiking, swim indoors, visit the beach, fish, or just relax here. Expensive. Highway 101, P.O. Box 118, Gleneden Beach, OR 97388. 503/764–2371, 800/547–6500 outside Oregon.

**Sunriver Lodge**—This exceptional resort is located on 3,300 lovely acres. It has two 18-hole golf courses, 22 tennis courts, canoeing, rafting, two swimming pools, horseback riding, biking on 25 miles of paved trails, and all the winter sports. There are 320 rooms, all very spacious and modern. Many of the rooms have jacuzzis and fireplaces. Expensive. P.O. Box 3609, Sun River, OR 97707. 503/593–1221.

**Yellow Point Lodge**—Call it camp for adults. This resort offers tennis, a swimming pool, windsurfing, a 32-foot boat for cruises, lawn games, a hot tub, and sauna. Guests stay in 52 comfortable rooms, located in the lodge or cabins. The cabins are more interesting, offering wood stoves and beds with tree-trunk bases. Expensive. RR3, Ladysmith, BC V0R 2E0. 604/245–7422.

Skykomish is also close to two popular lake areas. Dorothy Lakes is a series of four subalpine lakes connected by a nine-mile trail. Take the Miller River Road, three miles west of Skykomish, and drive ten miles south to the lakes. The other is Foss Lakes, a five-lake group connected by a six-mile trail. You can find these lakes by taking the Foss River Road two miles east of Skykomish.

Thirty miles east of Skykomish is Coles Corner and the turn-off for Lake Wenatchee, a popular fishing area in a wilderness region that also attracts skiers, hikers, and backpackers.

The next major attraction is Leavenworth, an alpine sawmill town that in the early 1960s decided to transform itself into a Bavarian village. This thematic conversion ranges from the acceptable Bavarian-cuisine restaurants (Baren Haus, Reiner's Gasthaus) and Bavarian-named hotels (Der Ritterhof, Edelweiss) to the ridiculous—a laundromat called Die Washerie.

The next stop is Highway 97, which you can take south to connect with I-90 or north to connect with Highway 20.

**I-90**—The fastest of the three Cascades highways passes through some fascinating landscape, but nothing that compares with the wonders seen on Highways 20 or 2. Although it is the least scenic, this route does have its charms. This includes the dramatic Snoqualmie Falls, four miles north of the town of North Bend via Highway 202. The 268-foot falls power a generating plant and can be seen from a pleasant park overlook. The Salish Inn is an excellent place for lunch or dinner at the terrace tables overlooking the waterfall.

North Bend has a ranger office for the Mt. Baker-Snoqualmie National Forest and the Snoqualmie Valley Historical Museum, which examines pioneer life in the 1800s as well as displays Indian artifacts.

The Puget Sound & Snoqualmie Valley Railroad offers wonderfully scenic 10-mile sightseeing trips through the region, passing near the Snoqualmie Falls. Catch the train at the depot on Highway 202 in Snoqualmie or at North Bend and Main Street in North Bend.

East of North Bend is the Snoqualmie Pass, a popular ski resort area, and the Alpine Lakes Wilderness, a protected area popular with hikers, campers, and anglers. Beyond the wilderness are two former mining towns—Cle Elum and Roslyn. Both are worth a visit before you connect with Highway 97 and go north to make a loop with Highways 2 or 20, or just turn around and return via I-5.

Cle Elum's top attraction, such as it is, is the Cle Elum Historic Telephone Museum at First and Wright streets. Roslyn's claim to fame are its many turn-of-the-century homes that have been renovated and turned into weekend retreats or shops and restaurants.

# For More Information

## On the Olympic Peninsula:

**Olympic Peninsula Travel Association**—c/o Washington State Ferries, Seattle Ferry Terminal, Pier 52, Seattle, WA 98104.

**Olympic National Park Headquarters**—600 East Park Avenue, Port Angeles, WA 98362. 206/452–4501.

**Olympic National Forest Headquarters**—801 S Capitol Way, Box 2288, Olympia, WA 98507. 206/753–9535.

## On the Long Beach Peninsula:

**Long Beach Visitors Bureau**—Seaview, WA 98644. 206/642–2400, 800/451–2542 in Washington.

## On the Oregon Coast:

**Astoria Chamber of Commerce**—111 W Marine Drive, Astoria, OR 97103. 503/325–6311.

**Brookings Harbor Chamber of Commerce**—97949 Shopping Center Avenue, Brookings, OR 97415. 503/469–3181.

**Cannon Beach Chamber of Commerce**—Second and Spruce streets, Cannon Beach, OR 97110. 503/436–2623.

**Florence Area Chamber of Commerce**—270 Highway 101, Florence, OR 97439. 503/997–3128.

**Greater Newport Chamber of Commerce—**555 SW Coast Highway, Newport, OR 97365. 503/265–8801, 800/262–7844.

**Oregon Dunes National Recreation Area—**Park Headquarters, 84505 Highway 101, Florence, OR 97439. 503/997–3641.

**Seaside Visitors Bureau—**7 N Roosevelt Avenue, Seaside, OR 97138. 503/738–6391.

**Tillamook Chamber of Commerce—**3705 Highway 101 N, Tillamook, OR 97141. 503/842–7525.

## On the Oregon Trail:

**Baker County Visitors and Convention Bureau—**490 Campbell Street, Baker City, OR 97814. 503/523–5855, 800/523–1235.

**Hells Canyon National Recreation Area—**2535 Riverside Drive, Clarkston, WA 99403. 509/758–8618.

**La Grande Chamber of Commerce—**2111 Adams Street, La Grande, OR 97850. 503/963–8588.

**Pendleton Chamber of Commerce—**25 SE Dorion Street, Pendleton, OR 97801. 800/452–9403 in Oregon, 800/547–8911 outside the state.

## For the Rocky Mountaineer:

**Rocky Mountaineer Railtours—**800/665–7245.

## On the Washington Cascades:

**City of North Bend—**P.O. Box 896, 211 Main Avenue, North Bend, WA 98045. 206/888–1211.

**Leavenworth Chamber of Commerce—**226 Eighth Street, Leavenworth, WA 98826. 206/548–5807.

**Mt. Baker-Snoqualmie National Forest—**915 Second Avenue, Seattle, WA 98104. 206/728–9696.

**North Cascades National Park—**2105 Highway 20, Sedro Woolley, WA 98282. 206/856–5700.

**Okanogan National Forest—**P.O. Box 950, Okanogan, WA 98840. 206/422–2704.

# *Where and When*

## *Olympic Peninsula:*

**Arthur D. Feiro Marine Laboratory Aquarium**—Port Angeles City Pier. Open 10:00 AM to 8:00 PM daily June through August; noon to 4:00 PM weekends the rest of the year. 206/452-9277.

**Clallam County Historical Museum**—Fourth and Lincoln Streets, Port Angeles. Open 10:00 AM to 4:00 PM Monday through Saturday from June through August; 10:00 AM to 4:00 PM weekdays the rest of the year. 206/452-7831.

**Dungeness National Widlife Refuge**—Kitchen Road, west of Sequim. Open daily. 206/683-5847.

**Hoh Visitor Center**—Hoh Road, 1.5 miles north of the Hoh River Bridge. The center is 20 miles off Highway 101. Open 9:00 AM to 7:00 PM daily June through August; 9:00 AM to 5:00 PM daily September through May. 206/374-6925.

**Olympic National Park Visitor Center**—3002 Mt. Angeles Road, Port Angeles. Open 9:00 AM to 4:00 PM daily. 206/452-4501.

**Sequim-Dungeness Museum**—175 W Cedar Street, Sequim. Open noon to 4:00 PM Wednesday through Sunday from May to September; noon to 4:00 PM weekends October, November, and mid-February through April. Closed the rest of the year. 206/683-8110.

**Sequim Natural History Museum**—503 N Sequim Avenue. Open noon to 4:00 PM Wednesday, Saturday, and Sunday. Closed December through mid-February.

**Sol Duc Hot Springs**—Soleduck Road and Highway 101. Open 9:00 AM to 9:00 PM daily mid-May through September. 206/327-3583.

## *Long Beach Peninsula:*

**Fort Canby State Park**—Highway 101, 2.5 miles south of Ilwaco. Open daily 6:30 AM to dusk April through October; 8:00 AM to dusk the rest of the year. 206/642-3078, 800/562-0990.

**Leadbetter State Park**—Robert Gray Drive, two miles south of Ilwaco. Open dawn to dusk April through October; 9:00 AM to dusk the rest of the year. 206/642–3078.

**Lewis & Clark Interpretive Center**—Fort Canby State Park. Open 9:00 AM to 5:00 PM daily Memorial Day through Labor Day; 10:00 AM to 3:00 PM weekends the rest of the year. 206/642–3078.

## *The Oregon Coast:*

**Blue Heron French Cheese Company**—2001 Blue Heron Drive, Tillamook. Open 8:00 AM to 8:00 PM daily in the summer; 9:00 AM to 5:00 PM daily the rest of the year. 503/842–8281.

**Columbia River Maritime Museum**—17th Street near Marine Drive, Astoria. Open 9:30 AM to 5:00 PM daily. Closed Mondays in winter. 503/325–2323.

**Darlingtona Botanical Wayside**—Mercer Lake Road, east of Highway 101 seven miles south of Heceta Head. Open daily.

**Flavel House/Heritage Museum**—441 Eighth Street, Astoria. Open 10:00 AM to 5:00 PM daily May through September; 11:00 AM to 4:00 PM daily the rest of the year. 503/325–2203.

**Ft. Clatsop National Memorial**—Highway 101 six miles south of Astoria. Open 8:00 AM to 6:00 PM daily June 10 through Labor Day; 8:00 AM to 5:00 PM daily the rest of the year. 503/861–2471.

**Hatfield Marine Science Center**—2030 Marine Science Drive, Newport. Open 9:30 AM to 6:00 PM in the summer; 10:00 AM to 4:00 PM the rest of the year. 503/867–3011.

**Oregon Dunes National Recreation Area**—Park headquarters, 84505 Highway 101, Florence. 503/997–3641.

**Pioneer Museum**—2016 Second Street, Tillamook. Open 8:00 AM to 5:00 PM Tuesday through Saturday; noon to 5:00 PM from October through March 15. 503/842–4553.

**Sea Gulch**—Highway 101, Seal Rock. Open 8:00 AM to 5:00 PM daily. 503/563–2727.

**Sunset Bay State Park**—13030 Cape Arago Highway, Charleston. Open 8:00 AM to dusk daily. 503/888–4902.

**Undersea Gardens**—250 SW Bay Boulevard, Newport. Open 9:00 AM to 8:00 PM daily mid-June through Labor Day; 10:00 AM to 5:00 PM daily the rest of the year. 503/265–2206.

## The Oregon Trail:

**Eastern Oregon Museum**—Nine miles south of Baker City on Highway 30 in Haines. Open 9:00 AM to 5:00 PM daily April through October. 503/523–5835.

**Hamley's Western Store**—30 SE Court, Pendleton. Call for hours. 503/276–2321.

**Oregon Trail Regional Museum**—2490 Grove Street, Baker City. Open 9:00 AM to 4:00 PM daily. 503/523–9308.

**Round-Up Hall of Fame**—SW Court at 13 Street, Pendleton. Tours on weekdays. 503/276–2553. (The Round-Up is the second full weekend in September.)

**Sumpter Valley Railroad**—30 miles southwest of Baker City on Highway 7. 503/894–2268.

**Vert Museum**—SW Fourth Street between Dorian and Emigrant streets, Pendleton. Open by appointment after the Round-Up from September to Memorial Day. 503/276–6924.

**Wallowa County Museum**—Highway 82, Joseph. Open 10:00 AM to 5:00 PM Memorial Day to September 16. 503/432–1015.

## Washington Cascades:

**Puget Sound & Snoqualmie Valley Railroad**—April to October. Ten-mile scenic tours, departing from the depot in Snoqualmie or North Bend. 206/746–4025.

**Skagit Tours Office**—Tours Thursdays through Mondays mid-June to Labor Day. City Lights Building, 1015 Third Avenue, Seattle, WA 98104. 206/684–3030.

# Romantic Retreats

Here are our favorite places to stay and dine. But first, an explanation of our cost categories:

One night in a hotel, resort, or inn for two:

*Inexpensive*—Less than $75.
*Moderate*—$75 to $125.
*Expensive*—More than $125.

Dinner for two (wine and drinks not included):

*Inexpensive*—Less than $25.
*Moderate*—$25 to $50.
*Expensive*—More than $50.

# The Long Beach Peninsula:

## Bay Center: Fine Dining

**Blue Heron Inn**—Oyster omelets and other great fresh seafood at this casual cafe in the fishing village of Bay Center. Inexpensive. Water Street. 206/875–9990.

## Chinook: Fine Dining

**The Sanctuary**—Swedish and Italian cuisine served in a renovated church. The fresh seafood dishes are the stars of this menu. Moderate. Hazel Street. 206/777–8380.

## Ilwaco: Romantic Lodging

**The Inn at Ilwaco**—Located in the old Presbyterian Church Sunday School, this nine-bedroom B&B offers plush accommodations. The church is used as an arts center and local theater. Moderate. 120 Williams Street NE, P.O. Box 922, Ilwaco, WA 98624–0922. 208/642–8686.

## Moclips: Romantic Lodging

**Ocean Crest Resort**—This 45-room resort commands a grand view of the ocean from its bluff setting. The rooms are pleasant and spacious, with fireplaces and great views. Facilities include a pool, jacuzzi, and weight room. Moderate. Highway

109, 18 miles north of Ocean Shore. Moclips, WA 98562. 206/276-4465.

## Seaview: Romantic Lodging

**The Shelburne Inn**—This 90-year-old inn in Seaview offers 16 rooms, all very nicely decorated but not all created equal. Avoid the rooms on the busy highway or those on the third floor in the summer. The best are the five rooms recently added on the west side. Moderate. P.O. Box 250, Seaview, WA 98644. 206/642-2442.

## Seaview: Fine Dining

**Shoalwater Restaurant**—This elegant dining room at the fine Shelburne Inn in Seaview features exceptional Northwest cuisine, with an emphasis on the fresh local seafood. Expensive. Pacific Highway 103 and 45th Street. 206/642-4142.

# The Olympic Peninsula:

## Aberdeen: Fine Dining

**Misty's**—Innovative cuisine featuring intriguing soups and salads and creative pastas and seafoods. Moderate. 116 W Heron Street. 206/533-0956.

## Forks: Romantic Lodging

**Manitou Lodge**—This remote log lodge is a stunning retreat offering four guest rooms and lots of quiet. There's great fishing in the nearby Soleduck and Bogachiel rivers. Inexpensive. (Call for directions.) P.O. Box 600, Forks, WA 98331. 206/374-6295.

**Kalaloch Lodge**—You have a choice of an old or new cabin, or rooms in an old lodge or new hotel. Choose the newest rooms or new log cabins. The rooms in the new hotel have fireplaces and decks, while the rooms in the original lodge are pleasant but have little to recommend, save some fantastic views. The cabins range from drafty and simple (old) to pleasant and simple (new). Moderate rooms, expensive cabins. HC 80, Box 1100, Forks-Kalaoch, WA 98331. 206/962–2271.

## Port Angeles: Romantic Lodging

**Lake Crescent Lodge**—This rustic 1915 cedar-and-fir landmark operated by the park service offers 42 rooms in motel units, the old lodge, or in four cabins, all located amid some fantastic scenery. Go for the cabins or the motel rooms. Inexpensive. Twenty miles west of Port Angeles on Highway 101, HC 62, Box 11, Port Angeles, WA 98362. 206/928–3211.

## Port Angeles: Fine Dining

**C'est Si Bon**—Outstanding French cuisine matched by the stunning views of a rose garden and the Olympic Mountains. The seafood dishes are excellent. Expensive. 2300 Highway 101 E. 206/452–8888

## Quinault: Romantic Lodging

**Lake Quinault Lodge**—This 89-room lodge sits next to a glacial lake in the majestic Olympic National Forest. The location is breathtaking, and the rooms are pleasant. Facilities include an indoor pool, jacuzzi, sauna, golf course, and games room. Expensive. S Shore Road, Box 7, Quinault, WA 98575. 206/288–2571.

## Sequim: Romantic Lodging

**Groveland Cottage**—Simple but comfortable rooms in a 90-year-old house near the Dungeness Spit. Moderate. 1673 Sequim Dungeness Way, Dungeness, WA 98382. 206/683–3565.

**Juan de Fuca Cottages**—Five cozy cottages, four of which overlook the Dungeness Spit and the fifth faces the Olympic Mountains. Moderate 561 Marine Drive, Sequim, WA 98382. 206/683–4433.

## Sequim: Fine Dining

**Casoni's**—Excellent Italian cuisine, featuring seafood, is served at this unpretentious place. Don't miss the killer desserts. Moderate. 104 Hooker Road. 206/683–2415.

**Eclipse Cafe**—Excellent Cambodian fare (a nice change from all that salmon and crab) served in a casual cafe. Inexpensive. 144 S Fifth Street. 206/683–2760 (reservations advised).

**The Oak Table**—Huge omelets and fruit crepes at breakfast and excellent quiches and sandwiches at lunch are served in this cute cottage. Inexpensive. Third and Bell streets. 206/683–2179.

**Scarborough Fayre**—It's a bit out of place, this Tudor building that houses a traditional English restaurant. It's wonderful. Don't miss the steak and kidney pie, cornish pastries, and other delights. Inexpensive. 126 E Washington Street. 206/683–7861.

**Three Crabs**—Avoid the deep-fried dishes and go for the crack-it-yourself Dungeness crab from October to April. Moderate. 101 Three Crabs Road. 206/683–4264.

(For more lodging and dining choices, see the Port Townsend section of Chapter 1.)

# The Kitsap Peninsula:

## Gig Harbor: Romantic Lodging

**Old Glencove Hotel**—This charming Victorian offers two suites and two rooms, all with great views of the small cove. The grounds are beautifully landscaped and are a popular place for parties and weddings. Moderate. 9418 Glencove Road, Gig Harbor, WA 98335. 206/884–2835.

## Poulsbo: Romantic Lodging

**Manor Farm Inn** —This lavish working farm offers eight excellent guest rooms, all nicely furnished with French country antiques. Two rooms have fireplaces. Facilities include a hot tub, large amounts of serenity, and horses, sheep, cows, and a trout pond. Excellent breakfast and dinners, too. Expensive. 26069 Big Valley Road NE, Poulsbo, WA 98370. 206/779–4628.

## Poulsbo: Fine Dining

**Larry's Best BBQ**—The decor isn't much (cow skulls, snakeskin, old mall location) but the barbecue is superb. Inexpensive. 19559 Viking Way. 206/697–BEST.

**Manor Farm Inn**—Outstanding five-course meals served only on weekends at this excellent B&B. There is one seating, at 6:30 PM and reservations are required. Expensive. 26069 Big Valley Road NE. 206/779–4628.

## Silverdale: Romantic Lodging

**Silverdale on the Bay Resort**—This 151-room resort has all the amenities a fine hotel needs: tastefully decorated rooms that have balconies, an indoor pool, sauna, boat dock, and exercise room. Moderate. The seafood is wonderful in the hotel dining room. 3073 Bucklin Hill Road, Silverdale, WA 98383. 206/698–1000.

# The Oregon Coast:

## Astoria: Romantic Lodging

**Franklin House**—This renovated Victorian B&B offers five spacious guest rooms. Avoid the one in the basement; it's big but a bit gloomy. The bridal suite is the nicest. Moderate. 1681 Franklin Avenue, Astoria, OR 97103. 503/325–5044.

**Franklin Street Station**—This turn-of-the-century building is a marvel of woodwork. The five guestrooms are furnished with Victorian pieces and decorated with beautiful local art. Moderate. 1140 Franklin Avenue, Astoria, OR 97103. 503/325–4314.

**Grandview Bed & Breakfast**—This huge mansion has three attractive guest rooms and three pleasant two-bedroom suites. Moderate. 1574 Grand Avenue, Astoria, OR 97103. 503/325–5555, 800/488–3250.

## Astoria: Fine Dining

**Pier 11 Feed Store**—Spacious and elegant, this dining room overlooks the Columbia River and features fine beef and seafood. Moderate. 11th Street at the river. 503/325–0279.

## Bandon: Fine Dining

**Bandon Boatworks**—Romantic waterfront restaurant that serves some of the finest seafood and steaks on the coast. Moderate. South Jetty Road. 503/347-2111.

## Cannon Beach: Romantic Lodging

**Surfview Resort**—Close to the scenic Haystack Rock, this attractive cedar-shake motel offers 129 spacious and comfortable rooms. Facilities include an indoor heated pool, sauna, hot tubs, and weight room. Expensive. 1400 S Hemlock Street, P.O. Box 547, Cannon Beach, OR 97110. 503/436-1566, 800/345-5676.

**Tern In Bed and Breakfast**—There are two spacious and attractive rooms in this B&B, which is in a quiet section of Cannon Beach. Moderate. 3663 S Hemlock Street, P.O. Box 952, Cannon Beach, OR 97110. 503/436-1528.

## Cannon Beach: Fine Dining

**The Bistro**—Flower boxes, background music, an herb garden, and outstanding Northwestern cuisine make this restaurant perhaps the best on the coast. Expensive. 263 N Hemlock Street. 503/436-2661.

**Cafe de la Mer**—This upscale, cozy restaurant features superb fresh seafood, pasta, and desserts. Expensive. 1287 S Hemlock Street. 503/436-1179.

## Charleston: Fine Dining

**Portside**—This casual dining room at the marina features fresh seafood, all caught that day aboard the restaurant's own boat. Moderate. 8001 Kingfisher Road. 503/888-5544.

## Cloverdale: Romantic Lodging

**Hudson House Bed & Breakfast**—This attractive historic house offers four nice guest rooms, all with bucolic views of the farm across the way. Moderate. 37700 Highway 101 S, Cloverdale, OR 97112. 503/392-3533.

### Coos Bay: Romantic Lodging

**This Olde House B&B**—This huge Victorian is crammed full of antiques and collectibles gathered by its owners over the years. There are four attractive rooms, which serve almost as display areas for many of their best finds. Moderate. 202 Alder Avenue, Coos Bay, OR 97420. 503/267–5224.

### Coos Bay: Fine Dining

**Blue Heron Bistro**—Excellent seafood and pastas served in an attractive and colorful dining room. The breakfasts here are wonderful! Moderate. 100 Commercial Street. 503/267–3933.

### Depoe Bay: Romantic Lodging

**The Inn at Otter Crest**—The grounds are beautifully landscaped and the 115 rooms and suites are spacious. Be sure to ask for one with a magnificent view of the ocean. Facilities include indoor and outdoor tennis and a nearby golf course. Expensive. P.O. Box 50, Otter Rock, OR 97369. 503/765–2111, 800/547–2181 outside Oregon.

### Florence: Romantic Lodging

**Johnson House Bed & Breakfast**—This beautiful Victorian home has five attractive guest rooms. Insiders, however, ask for the two cottages, one called the Coast House on the shore ten miles north, and the other named Moonset, facing Like Lake about nine miles away. Moderate. 216 Maple Street, P.O. Box 1892, Florence, OR 97439. 503/997–8000.

### Florence: Fine Dining

**Windward Inn**—This elegant restaurant features excellent seafood. Moderate. 3757 Highway 1091 N. 503/997–8243.

### Gleneden Beach: Romantic Lodging

**Salishan Lodge**—One of the most famous lodges in the Northwest, this magnificent, 200-room resort offers posh accommodations in eight-plex units located around the resort's 18-hole golf course. Rooms have fireplaces, balconies, local art, and great views of the grounds. You can golf, play tennis, go hiking, visit the beach, fish, or just relax here. Expensive. Highway 101, P.O. Box 118, Gleneden Beach, OR 97388. 503/764–2371, 800/547–6500 outside Oregon.

## *Gleneden Beach: Fine Dining*

**Chez Jeanette**—Flowers, fireplaces, antiques, and a setting in a forest make this inn a special place. The cuisine is French provincial, with a touch of the Northwest. Stick with the fresh seafood. Expensive. 7150 Old Highway 101. 503/764–3434.

**Salishan Lodge**—The fare at the dining room at this posh resort is uneven; your best bet is to stick to the fresh seafood. Expensive. Highway 101. 503/764–2371.

## *Gold Beach: Romantic Lodging*

**Fair Winds Bed and Breakfast**—This charming home offers one pleasant guest room. The wonderful setting is in a forest, with gardens and a gazebo with a jacuzzi on the grounds. Inexpensive. P.O. Box 1274, Gold Beach, OR 97444. 503/247–6753 (call for directions).

**Ireland's Rustic Lodges**—Spectacular location on a bluff overlooking the sea makes this place a real find. There are eight simple but cozy cabins and 27 rooms in a modern motel. Choose the cabins. Moderate. 1120 S Ellensburg Avenue, Gold Beach, OR 97444. 503/247–7718.

**Tu Tu Tun Lodge**—Located seven miles inland on the north shore of the Rogue River, this attractive lodge, one of the best in the Northwest, offers 16 pleasant rooms. The lodge has a pitch-and-putt golf course, lawn games, and excellent fishing. The jet boats that tour the river stop here to pick up passengers. Expensive. 96550 North Bank Rogue, Gold Beach, OR 97444. 503/247–6664.

## Lincoln City: Fine Dining

**Bay House**—Innovative cuisine, with unusual touches from France and the American Southwest in the dishes served at this prized dining room. Expensive. 5911 SW Highway 101. 503/996-3222.

## Manzanita: Fine Dining

**Blue Sky Cafe**—Nouvelle cuisine, emphasizing pastas and seafood, are served at this chic cafe—great breakfasts, too. Moderate. 154 Laneda Avenue. 503/368-5712.

## Newport: Romantic Lodging

**Oar House Bed & Breakfast**—Once a bordello (catch the pun?), this huge inn has only two guest rooms, decorated with a nautical theme. The inn has an indoor spa and sauna. Moderate. 520 SW Second Street, Newport, OR 97365. 503/265-9571.

**Ocean House Bed & Breakfast**—The oceanfront setting is spectacular and the charm and warmth at this four-room inn are legendary. Moderate. 4920 NW Woody Way, Newport, OR 97365. 503/265-6158.

**Sylvia Beach Hotel**—This grand blufftop hotel has 20 charming rooms, each decorated in a whimsical style and named after literary figures. Moderate. 267 NW Cliff Street, Newport, OR 97365. 503/265-5428.

## Newport: Fine Dining

**Canyon Way Restaurant**—This bookstore and gift shop is also a fine restaurant serving pasta and seafood. Moderate. 1216 SW Canyon Way. 503/265-8319.

**Tables of Content**—An award-winner for the name alone, this pleasant restaurant at the Sylvia Beach features excellent seafood. Moderate. 267 NW Cliff Street. 503/265-5428.

**The Whale's Tale**—Great seafood at dinner, vegetarian fare at lunch at this popular dining room. Moderate. 452 SW Bay Boulevard. 503/265-8660.

## Oceanside: Romantic Lodging

**Three Capes Bed and Breakfast**—There are two spacious and attractively furnished guest rooms in this contemporary house. Moderate. 1685 Maxwell Mountain Road, Oceanside, OR 97134. 503/842-6126.

## Oceanside: Fine Dining

**Roseanna's**—Excellent seafood, served with live music in the evening. Moderate. 1440 Pacific. 503/842-7351.

## Port Orford: Romantic Lodging

**Gilbert Inn B&B**—This elegant Queen Anne Victorian has ten antique-filled rooms that are wonderful. Moderate. 341 Beach Drive, Port Orford, OR 97138. 503/739-9770.

## Port Orford: Fine Dining

**The Whale Cove**—Great ocean views, and a wonderful menu that usually reflects the Russian and Irish and artistic flair of chef Michael Petchekovitch. The fresh local seafood and game dishes are the best choices. Moderate. 190 Sixth Street (Highway 101 S). 503/332-7575.

## Waldport: Romantic Lodging

**Cliff House Bed & Breakfast**—Perched on a bluff over-looking miles of beach, this romantic inn has five lovely guest rooms, each with a balcony. The bridal suite has a skylight, a jacuzzi, and a totally mirrored bathroom. Facilities include a sauna and hot tub. Moderate. P.O. Box 436, Waldport, OR 97394. 503/563-2506.

## Yachats: Romantic Lodging

**Adobe Motel**—There are 56 pleasant and attractive rooms in this oceanfront hotel. Facilities include a jacuzzi and sauna. The bar is a great place to sit and watch the passing whales in March and April. Moderate. 1555 Highway 101, Yachats, OR 97498. 503/547-3141.

**Ziggurat**—This four-story, glass and wood pyramid is a stunning beach house. Named after a Sumerian pyramid in Babylon, this house has two guest rooms that share a bathroom and sauna. Guests share the spacious first-floor living area. Moderate. 95330 Highway 101, Yachats, OR 97498. 503/547–3925.

## *The Oregon Trail:*

Lodging is limited in this sparsely populated region of eastern Oregon. Here is the best:

### *Adams: Romantic Lodging*

**Bar M Ranch**—Once a stagecoach stop more than a century ago, this rustic ranch in the beautiful Blue Mountains offers riding, guided overnight trips, and a perfect base to explore eastern Oregon. Guests stay in cabins, the main ranch house, and an annex. Rates are by the week, and costs start around $500 per person, all meals included. Route 1, Box 263, Adams, OR 97810. 503/566–3381. Open May through September.

### *Baker City: Romantic Lodging*

**Best Western Sunridge Inn**—We rarely recommend standard motels, but this is an excellent Best Western and the nicest lodging in the area. Moderate. 1 Sunridge Lane, Baker City, OR 97814. 503/523–6444.

### *Baker City: Fine Dining*

**Anthony's**—Unusual decor and intimate surroundings make this restaurant a certain conversation starter. Excellent seafood dishes. Moderate. 1926 First Street. 503/523–4475.

### *Joseph: Romantic Lodging and Fine Dining*

**Wallowa Lake Lodge**—There are 31 units at this simple 1920s lodge in Wallowa State Park near Joseph. The best rooms are in the eight cottages. The dining room at this historic lodge features fine seafood and local game dishes. Moderate. Box 320, Route 1, Joseph, OR 97846. 503/432–9821.

### La Grande: Romantic Lodging

**Stange Manor Bed and Breakfast—**This plush but unpretentious house was built by a lumber baron. It now offers five pleasant guest rooms, two of which share a sitting room with a fireplace. The best room is the master suite. Moderate. 1612 Walnut Street, La Grande, OR 97850. 503/963–2400.

### La Grande: Fine Dining

**Mamacita's—**Excellent Mexican food is served in a colorful adobe-walled room. Inexpensive. 110 Depot Street. 503/963–6223.

### Pendleton: Fine Dining

**Cimmiyotti's—**Great steaks and salads are served at this western-style restaurant. Moderate. 137 S Main Street. 503/276–4314.

## The Washington Cascades:

### Cle Elum: Romantic Lodging

**The Moore House—**The railraod memorabilia—photos, model trains, and other artifacts—are meant to remember the railway workers who stayed here long ago. There are ten rooms in the bunkhouse. The rooms are pleasant and furnished with antique reproductions. The caboose may be the most romantic for train buffs. It has a queen-sized bed, private sundeck, bath, and refrigerator. Facilities include an outdoor hot tub. Moderate. 526 Marier Avenue, South Cle Elum, WA 98943. 206/674–5939.

### Cle Elum: Fine Dining

**Mama Vallone's Steak House—**Great steaks and pasta are served at this friendly dining room. Moderate. 302 W First Street. 509/674–5174.

## Concrete: Romantic Lodging

**Cascade Mountain Inn**—Six cozy guest rooms in a spacious log lodge in the Upper Skagit Valley make this a special mountain retreat. In the winter, the valley is a haven for bald eagles. Moderate. 3840 Pioneer Lane. Concrete, WA 98237. 206/826–4333.

## Leavenworth: Romantic Lodging

**Haus Rohrbach Pension**—This European-style pension has an alpine decor and great views of the valley. There are ten small but pleasant rooms, each with flower-decked balconies with views of the mountains. Moderate. 12882 Ranger Road, Leavenworth, WA 98826. 509/548–7024.

**Pension Anna**—Located in the center of the village, this small Austrian-style inn has 11 rooms decorated with antique pine furniture. Expensive. 926 Commercial Street, Leavenworth, WA 98826. 509/548–6273.

**Run of the River**—This log cabin has three pleasant rooms, facing the river and the wildlife refuge. Moderate. 9308 E Leavenworth Road, P.O. Box 448, Leavenworth, WA 98826. 509/548–7171.

## Leavenworth: Fine Dining

**Reiner's Gasthaus**—Austrian and Hungarian specialties are served European-style at shared tables. Inexpensive. 829 Front Street. 509/548–5111.

**Terrace Bistro**—Continental cuisine, with only a few German dishes on the menu. Moderate. 200 Eighth Street. 509/548–4193.

## Rockport: Romantic Lodging

**Diablo Lake Resort**—Eighteen pleasant rooms at this comfortable motel. Inexpensive. Rockport, WA 98283. 206/386–4429.

## Snohomish: Romantic Lodging

**Noris House**—The three guest rooms are spacious and attractive in this grand Edwardian inn in Snohomish's historic district. The breakfasts here are wonderful. Ask for the room with the fireplace and balcony. Moderate. 312 Avenue D, Snohomish, WA 98290. 206/568–3825.

## Snohomish: Fine Dining

**Peking Duck**—Terrific Szechwan dishes in an otherwise ugly location in a strip shopping center. Inexpensive. 1208 Second Avenue. 206/568–7634.

## Snoqualmie: Romantic Lodging

**Salish**—The setting next to a 268-foot-high waterfall is magnificent, but not all the rooms have this grand view. There are 83 attractive rooms and nine excellent suites. The suites face the falls. The 83 other rooms face upriver, with the power company's transformer station disrupting the view. Expensive. 37807 SE Fall City Road, Snoqualmie, WA 98065. 206/888–2556, 800/826–6124.

## Snoqualmie: Fine Dining

**Herbfarm**—This is the place to stop for lunch if the Salish lodge's dining room is too full or too expensive. Located in Falls City just a 10-minute drive from the falls, the Herbfarm offers excellent seafood, lamb, and salads. Open only April through December. Moderate. 32804 Issaquah–Fall City Road, Fall City. 206/784–2222.

**Salish**—The location is next to a 268-foot waterfall is magnificent, and the innovative Northwestern cuisine is sensational. The Salish is famous for its Sunday brunch. Expensive. 37807 SE Fall City Road. 206/888–2556.

## Winthrop: Romantic Lodging

**Sun Mountain Lodge**—Recently remodeled, this inn is popular with cross-country skiers who use the 50 miles of trails in the Methow Valley. The best rooms are the newest. Each has a fireplace and great view of the valley. Expensive. Patterson Lake Road, nine miles south of Winthrop. P.O. Box 1000, Winthrop, WA 98862. 509/996–2211.

**Farmhouse Inn**—This restored farmhouse offers six guest rooms, three of which are tiny. Ask for rooms one and two, or the two-bedroom suite. Moderate. (Register at the Duck Brand Hotel in Winthrop). Highway 20, outside of town. P.O. Box 118, Winthrop, WA 98862. 509/996–2191.

## *Winthrop: Fine Dining*

**Duck Brand Cantina and Hotel**—This is the best place for food in Winthrop, and the menu offers an exotic mixture of Mexican, Italian, and plain American cuisine. Inexpensive. 248 Riverside Avenue. 509/996–2192.

Alaska's mighty glaciers are an awe-inspiring sight. *(Photograph by Barbara Radin-Fox)*

CHAPTER **6**

# *Alaska: The Last Frontier*

*A*laska is a wild and wonderful land where, despite the oil drilling and tourism, you can still escape into an unspoiled wilderness.

Alaska is the largest state—586,412 square miles, 2½ times the size of Texas and one-fifth of all the land in the United States. Yet fewer than 600,000 people live within this vast territory, less than the population of the 87-square-mile District of Columbia.

Alaska is the land of gold and oil—riches that have driven mankind to endure incredible hardships in the quest for wealth. Alaska is also the land of ancient rituals, some longheld by the Eskimos and Indians who have lived here for centuries, and some part of nature's seasonal rhythms. Salmon come to spawn and the eagles gather to prey in Alaska, and whales as well as birds and fowl migrate here. It is a land of endless daylight and endless nights, of majestic mountains, and skies burning with heavenly fires.

Visiting Alaska requires a change in mindset for travelers. Distances are vast, towns often isolated and unreachable except by sea or air, and accommodations are often simple or rustic. We have broken this chapter into two parts, Southeastern Alaska and Central Alaska, to help you find your way to the major attractions.

Southeastern Alaska is the region visitors know best, for it is the main route traveled by cruise ships. In this region, you will find mountains, glaciers, lush forests, and fjords, as well as Juneau, the state capital, and Sitka, the ancient Russian capital. Here also are fishing villages, gold rush towns, and Indian settlements.

Central Alaska is where you find Mt. McKinley and the state's two major cities—Anchorage and Fairbanks. This part of Alaska is incredibly beautiful but the distances—Juneau and Anchorage are 600 miles apart—are often challenging. Group tours are the best ways to experience the wonders of central Alaska, unless you are an experienced, self-sufficent traveler. For more details on tour groups, see the box on page 181.

## Southeastern Alaska

Southeastern Alaska is a thin slice of mainland and more than a thousand islands—some of which are one hundred miles long—that make up the Alexander Archipelago. This region, a bit more than 500 miles long and as much as 140 miles wide, is a maze of thickly forested islands teeming with wildlife, glacier-carved mountains, mysterious fjords, and isolated towns and villages. Southeast Alaska has a climate distinctly different from that of the rest of the state. It rains more than 150 inches a year in some spots—and the temperatures rarely reach above the 60s or fall below the 20s.

You can only tour Southeast Alaska by air or water. The Inland Passage is the main street here, the route used by the Alaska Marine Highway ferries as well as cruise ships. Travelers can also use regular commercial air service or countless float planes that are the equivalent of taxis in this part of the world. There are no roads connecting the towns, and the few miles of road that exist usually come to a dead end just outside of town.

The cities here are small. Juneau, the capital, has only 30,000 residents, yet it is the third largest city in the state behind Anchorage and Fairbanks. Ketchikan has 13,000 residents and ranks fourth in size. There are five cities well worth visiting here, three on the mainland and two on the islands. The mainland attractions are Juneau, Haines, and Skagway; the island cities are Ketchkian and Sitka. Here are their profiles:

**Haines**—Naturalist John Muir and missionary S. Hall Young founded this town in 1879 as a mission for the Alaskan Indians. Today Haines is a seacoast community best known as the starting point of the Alaska Highway.

Start a tour at the marker for Mile 0 on the Haines Highway at Front Street, the starting point for the road to Alaska and

Canada's Yukon. The famed highway divides Haines into two different neighborhoods. South of the highway is the former Fort Seward, which was closed after World War II, sold, and renamed Port Chilkoot. The fort's buildings and officers' homes have been restored and now house the Alaska Indian Arts Skill Center—where you can see Indian artists carving totems, creating masks, and working on jewelry in the old hospital (building No. 13). On the parade grounds is a recreated Tlingit village with an Indian tribal house, totem poles, and a sourdough log cabin. The Chilkat Center for the Arts, behind the hospital, holds dances in the evenings performed by elaborately costumed Chilkat Indians.

North of the Haines Highway is the town founded by Muir and Young. The Haines Visitor Center at Second and Willard streets has some maps for walking tours. The top attractions in this part of Haines are the interesting exhibits on Indians and pioneers at the Sheldon Museum and Cultural Center on Main Street near the harbor.

For shopping, visit the Northern Arts Gallery on Second Avenue or the Chilkat Valley Arts at 307 Willard Street. Both sell some excellent works by local artists.

**Juneau**—The state capital of Alaska is crammed between Mt. Juneau and the Gastineau Channel, giving it the appearance of a fishing village with a towering backyard. In 1880, Juneau became prime real estate when Joe Juneau and Dick Harris, two rarely sober prospectors, were led by the Tlingit Indian chief Kowee to a pool in the creek that courses through the town. The prospectors found that the bottom of the pool was paved with gold nuggets. The discovery set off a gold boom and the creation of a camp that became the capital of the Alaskan government, named after Joe Juneau.

Juneau today is a busy, sprawling city, with most of its population scattered miles from the camp site where it all began. Juneau streets are lined with bars and shops and the waterfront buzzes with motoring tour boats and constant takeoffs and landings of float planes.

Start a tour of the city at the waterfront's Marine Park. In the summer, the park's kiosk is staffed with tourism officials who answer questions about the city's history. You can also sign up for a trip to Juneau Icecap or Glacier Bay with one of the sea and air tour groups who have booths in the park.

Walk away from the waterfront park and you quickly enter the main shopping district. The area bordered by Second, Fifth, Franklin, and Main streets contains many shops selling furs, souvenirs, antiques, and art. Some of the better shops include the Alaskan Heritage Bookshop, at 174 S Franklin Street; Gallery of the Far North and the Mt. Juneau Trading Post, both at 147 S Franklin Street; Fairweather Gallery of Wearable Art, at 118 Seward Street; Artwork Unlimited, an artists' cooperative at 287 S Franklin Street; and AlasSkins Leather at 479 S Franklin Street; AlasSkins features leathers made from salmon, halibut, and sea bass. Outstanding works of art by Alaskans can be bought at Objects of Bright Pride, 165 S Franklin Street, while Russian lacquered boxes, icons, samovars, and other items from that country can be found at the Russian Shop on the second floor at 175 S Franklin Street.

Juneau also has attractions rich with history. The St. Nicholas Russian Orthodox Church at Fifth and Gold Streets was built in 1894 and is the oldest original Russian church in the state. Another historic building is the House of Wickersham at 213 Seventh Street. The house was the residence of James Wickersham, a judge and delegate to Congress. Built in 1899, the house has exhibits on Russian and pioneer life. Tours are offered during the summer.

The City Museum at Fourth and Main streets has some nice displays on the miners and early pioneers. It's one of two fine museums in town. The other is the Alaska State Museum a few blocks west at 319 Whittier Street, with exhibits on Native Alaskans, animals, and the miners.

Two other natural wonders are must-sees. Follow Gold Creek, the small stream that wanders through the town, into the hills until you come to the base of Mt. Juneau. You can pan for gold here or stay for a salmon-bake as part of a guided tour. The forest, only minutes from downtown Juneau, is a nearly untouched wilderness; the only signs of human life are the ruins of long-closed mining operations. In the summer, the face of Mt. Juneau cascades with waterfalls fed by the melting ice atop the mountain.

The other attraction is the Mendenhall Glacier, a river of blue ice 12 miles long and 1.5 miles wide. The glacier is 13 miles northwest of town via Highway 7 and the Mendenhall Loop Road. Trails lead you to some grand views of the glacier, part of the breathtaking Juneau Icefield.

Another exciting trip, a bit farther away, is a journey to Admiralty Island National Monument. The mountainous island is a million-acre wonderland, ranging from rain forests to snow-capped peaks. It's a wildlife paradise, with Alaskan brown bears outnumbering humans, as well as snow geese, otter, beaver, mink, Sitka black-tailed deer, and other rare animals. Floatplanes and ferries make the trip from Juneau to the island. You can also rent a rustic cabin from the forest service (details below).

**Ketchikan**—Located about 240 miles south of Juneau, Ketchikan prides itself on its weather—usually miserable—and its salmon fishing—usually outstanding.

This town, located on Deer Island next to the 3,000-foot Deer Mountain, gets more than 150 inches of rain a year. The locals explain the weather this way: "If you can't see the top of Deer Mountain, it's raining. If you can, it's going to rain."

Despite the weather, Ketchikan is an interesting seaport to visit. The salmon fishing is excellent, evidenced by the large fleet of sportfishing boats in its marinas, and the town itself has a certain rugged charm.

Start a tour at the Thomas Basin, the marina on the south end of town. The main road behind the basin is Sedman Street. Turn left and walk toward the bridge and Creek Street, one of Ketchikan's most colorful roads. Once a red-light district, its quaint houses built on stilts over the creek are now quaint shops. Creek Street's most famous brothel, Dolly's House, has been preserved as a museum. It is open only when cruise ships are in port.

Return to Sedman Street and cross the creek into town. The Tongass Historical Museum and Totem Pole at 629 Dock Street has an interesting collection of pioneer and Indian artifacts. Walk north and then turn east on Park Avenue to the salmon falls and fish ladder. These beautiful fish shimmy upstream to spawn in mid-summer and early fall, creating an incredible display.

Continue east on Park Avenue to the City Park and the Deer Mountain Hatchery, which raises King and Coho salmon. Just across the street is the Totem Heritage Center, which displays Indian carvings. Excellent examples of this unusual art form can be seen at Ketchikan's most famous attractions—Totem Bight State Historical Park, ten miles north of town on the North Tongass Highway, and the Saxman Indian Village, two miles south on the Tongass Highway. The Saxman Indian Village offers shows by the Cape Fox Dancers. Admission to see the dancers is about $30, $20 for just the village. Whether the dancers offer a show or not depends on the size of the audience—the larger the audience, the better the chances.

Tour groups offer trips to these sights and the nearby wilderness areas. The visitors' center at 131 Front Street can provide more information about current tour schedules and fees.

For shoppers, Ketchikan holds a few delights. Visit Tom Sawyer's at 306 Mission Street, for jewelry. The Tongass Trading Co. at 312 Dock Street and Authentic Alaska Craft at 318 Dock Street have interesting crafts, while the Scanlon Gallery at 310 Mission Street has some fine Alaskan art.

Ketchikan is also a popular place to catch a variety of tours. From the waterfront you can hire a captain to take you salmon fishing or sightseeing for eagles and other wildlife. The most popular destination is the Misty Fjords National Monument, a fascinating territory of rugged scenery and wildlife.

**Sitka**—Once an ancient settlement of the Tlingit Indians, this seaport surrounded by rugged forests was settled by Russian traders in 1799 and named New Archangel. After a fierce battle with the Indians, the Russians secured their outpost and established a thriving community dealing in furs, ice, and other products of the New World.

After the Russians turned over control of Alaska and Sitka to Americans in 1867, Sitka maintained elements of its Russian past.

Start a tour of this city at the Centennial Building on Harbor Drive, where you can see the New Archangel Dancers performing in costume. The Isabelle Miller Museum in the building displays a model of the original Russian fort and other relics from the past.

The high ground just west of the Centennial Building is called Castle Hill. This is where the Russian governors lived and where, on October 18, 1867, they officially turned the territory over to America. Russian cannons still guard the hill.

Across the street is Totem Square, where you can see a totem with a Czarist eagle carved into its surface. Walk into town and turn left on Lincoln Street and head for the gem of Sitka—St. Michael's Cathedral. This structure is almost an exact copy of the original building that was destroyed by fire in 1966. Thanks to heroic efforts by townspeople, the relics, icons, and other religious items were saved and are now displayed in the sanctuary.

Shopping in town is limited, but the Baranof Indian & Eskimo Arts at 237 Lincoln Street, across from St. Michael's, and the Russian–American Company in the Bayview Trading Mall at 407 Lincoln Street are well worth a visit.

You can find the final attractions in town by walking or riding west on Lincoln Street to the Sitka National Historical Park and its visitors' center. The center offers audiovisual programs and interesting exhibits on Russian and Indian life in Sitka and demonstrations by artists in the center's studios.

Outside the building are 28 Tlingit and Haida Indian totem poles. Some of the totems are almost a century old, and are among the finest in the state. Behind the totems is a marked trail leading to Fort Tlingit, the site of the decisive battle in 1804 in which the Russians overran the Tlingit stronghold and secured their domination of this part of the Northwest.

**Skagway**—As you walk down Broadway in Skagway you may ask yourself "What year is it?" The launching point for prospectors drawn by the 1897–98 Klondike Gold Rush, this town seems frozen in time. The hotels, false-front stores, saloons, and even brothels of the Gold Rush Era have been restored and preserved as a living museum to one of history's wildest gold rushes.

Start a visit of this colorful town by stopping at the Trail of '98 Museum at Seventh Avenue and Spring Street. Here you will find gambling artifacts from the Board of Trade Saloon, as well as papers and other artifacts from those golden days. Broadway is the center of Skagway's historic district, where the old buildings have been refurbished and reopened to attract tourists rather than prospectors. Corrington's Alaska Ivory Co. on Broadway between Fifth and Sixth Avenue and the Kirme's Curio Shop at Fifth and Broadway sell some excellent gifts, jewelry, and art.

One entertaining stop in this historic area is the Eagles Hall, at Broadway and Sixth Avenue, where local actors perform a show called "Skagway in the Days of '98," complete with dancing and gambling with fake money.

On Broadway between Second and Third is the odd-looking Arctic Brotherhood Hall, a fraternity of Arctic pioneers. The brotherhood decorated the building's exterior with 20,000 pieces of driftwood. The hall is now a theater, showing "The White Pass Railroad Story" daily.

Walk east on Second Avenue to the White Pass and Yukon Rail Depot, now the headquarters of the Klondike Gold Rush National Historical Park. The building has displays and artifacts from the gold rush. You can take a train tour of gold country by riding the White Pass & Yukon Route cars. The train departs from the station on Second Avenue at Spring Street.

## Central Alaska

Mainland Alaska is a vast wonderland, filled with mountains that seem to touch the sky, lush valleys bursting with color, and a wide variety of wildlife. Touring this region is best done with a tour group (see box on page 181).

# GUIDED TOURS OF ALASKA

Touring the countryside of Alaska is not for everyone. The distances can be vast, the wildlife scary, and the landscape and weather challenging. Here are some of the best groups to join for a guided tour:

**Alaska Heritage Tours**—Specializes in small group tours of the Coumbia Glacier, around Wrangell and circular drives from Anchorage. P.O. Box 210691, Anchorage, AK 99521-0691. 907/696-8687.

**Alaska Photographic and Adventure Tours**—Tours of Homer, Denali National Park, the Kenai Fjords, and other attractions. 1831 Kuskokwim Street, Suite 12, Anchorage, AK 99508. 907/276-3418.

**Alaska Wildland Adventures**—Natural history and sport-fishing safaris along the coast and in Denali National Park. Box 389, Girdwood, AK 99587. 800/334-8730.

**All Alaska Tours**—This group offers a wide range of air, land, and sea tours of the state's wonders. Box 389, Haines, AK 99827. 800/661-0468.

**Eagle Custom Tours**—Private charters and package tours designed around your interests. 329 F Street, Suite 206, Anchorage, AK 99501. 907/277-6228.

**Gray Line of Alaska**—The land partner of Holland-America Cruise Lines, this organization offers tours by motorcoach, train, boat and airplane almost everywhere in Alaska. 300 Elliott Avenue, Seattle, WA 98119. 800/544-2206.

**Marktours**—Year-round tours of the arctic, the parks, Prince William Sound, wildlife, and the northern lights. P.O. Box 196769, Anchorage, AK 99519-6769. 800/426-6784 outside Alaska, 800/478-0800 inside the state.

**Natural History Adventures**—Tours led by biologists, exploring flyway migrations, tundra flora, bears, caribou, and whales. 601 Fifth Avenue, Suite 550, Anchorage, AK 99501. 907/258-9742.

Here is an overview of the top attractions:

**Anchorage**—Located on a high bluff over two arms of the Cook Inlet, this modern city has 226,000 residents, half of Alaska's population. Anchorage, founded in 1914 as the construction base for the Alaskan Railroad, has a number of historic buildings. The city serves as an excellent base for starting out on explorations of the backcountry.

The major historic sites include two excellent museums. The Anchorage Museum of History and Art at 121 W Seventh Avenue explores the culture and history of Alaska. The Heritage Library and Museum at Northern Lights Boulevard and C Street displays Eskimo and Indian artifacts and relics from the Gold Rush days.

Homes that date back to Anchorage's early years can be found on Second Avenue. Visit the Andrew Christiansen House at 542 Second Avenue (he auctioned the first lots here), the Leopold David House at No. 605 (the first elected mayor) and the William Edes House at No. 610 (chairman of the Alaskan Engineering Commission).

For shopping, visit the Alaska Native Arts & Crafts Association, 333 W Fourth Avenue; the Anchorage Fur Factory, at 105 W Fourth Avenue; and the Alaska Heritage Arts, at 400 D Street, where native Alaskan artisans are frequently carving wood, bone, soapstone, and horn.

The wilder side of Alaska is examined in film at the Alaska Experience Theater, 705 W Sixth Avenue. The theater presents the movie "Alaska the Greatland," a 40-minute documentary on the great outdoors. The animals of Alaska can be seen safely at the Alaska Zoo, 7.5 miles south of town on Highway 1.

You can get a closer look at Alaska's splendors at the Chugach State Park, which borders Anchorage on all but the water side. Here you can spot wildlife, go cross-country skiing, take guided nature walks, or just enjoy the magnificent scenery.

Anchorage is also the departure point for wonderful sightseeing tours of Prince William Sound, Kodiak Island, Columbia Glacier, Denali National Park (see Chapter 4), and rafting and gold-panning trips on nearby rivers.

**Fairbanks**—Located almost in the center of the state, Fairbanks is a convenient departure point for touring Alaska's beautiful backcountry. Fairbanks is much smaller than Anchorage—only about 25,000 residents—but it is a busy town for those arriving by air to take tours of Denali, the Arctic, and other remote areas of the state.

Attractions within the city itself are few. The Fire House Theater at the Cripple Creek Resort offers shows on Alaska's interior through the seasonal changes and a fascinating show called "The Crown of Light," which recreates the aurora borealis (northern lights). The Malemute Saloon, also at the resort, is a colorful reminder of Fairbanks' pioneer days. The "Service With a Smile" performance retells the Gold Rush days in story and song, featuring the poems of Robert Service. The Cripple Creek Resort, a turn-of-the-century gold camp, is in Ester, eight miles west of Fairbanks.

Alaskaland, a theme park at Peger and Airport roads, offers another look at pioneer life. Don't dismiss Alaskaland as just another tourist attraction. It's actually a treasure-trove of Alaska's heritage. There you can find a Gold Rush-era town recreated from 29 cabins from Fairbanks' early years, the narrow-gauge Crooked Creek & Whiskey River Island Railroad, the Pioneer Air Museum, and a Kkaayah, a constructed Native American village. You can try your hand at gold panning or just enjoy the feast at a salmon bake.

The Gold Rush days are also remembered at Gold Dredge No. 8, a five-deck ship built in 1928 to mine the Engineer and Goldstream creeks for gold. The dredge, on Goldstream Road, off Highway 6 north of Fairbanks, is open for tours.

The University Museum on the campus of the University of Alaska, on the west side of town, features Native Alaskan arts and crafts and natural history displays.

For some outstanding Alaskan crafts, we suggest a visit to the Alaska Native Arts & Crafts Center of Fairbanks, at 1603 College Road, and the Arctic Traveler's Gift Shop at 201 Cushman Street.

**Kenai Fjords National Park**—This 580,000-acre park on the southeastern side of the Kenai Peninsula contains the Harding Icefield, one of the four largest in the United States. Incredibly, the icefield covers all but the top of the Kenai Mountains. The coastal waters are populated with whales, seals, porpoises, and otters. Visitor access is by plane, car, or boat from Seward or by air charter from other communities.

**Kodiak**—Established in 1792 by Russian fur traders, Kodiak still has a Russian orthodox church with the traditional onion-shaped domes. The attractions in town include the excellent Baranov Museum, a late seventeenth-century warehouse with displays of early Alaskan artifacts. Outside of town is the Kodiak National Wildlife Refuge, a 1.8-million acre reserve that is the natural habitat of the Kodiak bear, a gigantic animal that can weigh as much as 1,500 pounds. Kodiak Tours offers narrated visits to the refuge and the top sights in town.

## For More Information

**Alaska Tourism Marketing Council**—Dept. 901, P.O. Box 110801, Juneau, AK 99811–0801. 907/465–2010.

**Anchorage Convention and Visitors Bureau**—201 E Third Avenue, Anchorage, AK 99501. 907/276–4118.

**Fairbanks Convention and Visitor Bureau**—550 First Avenue, Fairbanks, AK 99701. 907/456–5774, 800/327–5774.

**Haines Visitor Information Center**—P.O. Box 518, Haines, AK 99827. 907/766–2202.

**Juneau**—Contact the Davis Log Cabin Information Center, 134 Third Street, Juneau, AK 99801. 907/586–2201.

**Kenai Fjords National Park**—P.O. Box 1727, Seward, AK 99664. 907/224–3175.

**Ketchikan Visitors Bureau**—131 Front Street, Ketchikan, AK 99901. 907/225–6166.

**Kodiak Visitor Information Center**—100 Marine Way, Kodiak, AK 99615. 907/486–4070.

**Mendenhall Glacier Visitor Center**—P.O. Box 2097, Juneau, AK 99803. 907/789-0097.

**Misty Fjords National Monument**—In the Tongass National Forest east of Ketchikan. Headquarters are at 1817 Tongass Avenue, P.O. Box 6137, Ketchikan, AK 99901. 907/225-2148.

**Sitka Convention and Visitors Bureau**—P.O. Box 1226, Sitka, AK 99835. 907/747-5940.

**Skagway Convention and Visitors Bureau**—P.O. Box 415, Skagway, AK 99840. 907/983-2854.

**U.S. Forest Service**—Centennial Hall, 101 Egan Drive, Juneau, AK 99801. 907/586-8751.

## *Where and When*

### *Anchorage:*

**Alaska Experience Theater**—705 W Sixth Avenue. Open 8:00 AM to 10:00 PM daily June through September; 10:00 AM to 9:00 PM weekdays; 11:00 AM to 8:00 PM weekends the rest of the year. 907/276-3730.

**Anchorage Museum of History and Art**—121 W Seventh Avenue. Guided tours at 11:00 AM and 2:00 PM. Open 9:00 AM to 6:00 PM Monday through Saturday (until 9:00 PM Tuesday and Thursday); 1:00 PM to 5:00 PM Sunday June through August; 9:00 AM to 6:00 PM Tuesday through Saturday the rest of the year. 907/264-4326.

**Chugach State Park**—Visitor center open 11:00 AM to 7:00 PM Friday through Monday during the summer. Call for winter hours. 907/345-5014.

**Heritage Library and Museum**—301 W Northern Lights Boulevard. Open noon to 4:00 PM weekdays. 907/265-2834.

### *Fairbanks:*

**Alaskaland**—Airport Way and Peger Road. Open 11:00 AM to 9:00 PM daily Memorial Day to Labor Day. 907/452-4529.

---

♣

# GETTING AROUND ALASKA

Traveling around Alaska isn't easy, but it can be an adventure and lots of fun! There are several choices, some of which are a bit more unusual than what one would find in most of the lower 48 states:

• The Alaska Marine Highway System operates ferries that can take you and your vehicle (if you have one) to various ports of call, including stops in Alaska, Washington state, and British Columbia. In southeastern Alaska, if you have a vehicle, it really is the only way to travel. It's a wonderful cruise as well as a pleasant way to travel. You can even book a stateroom if your destination is far enough away. Call or write Alaska Marine Highway, Box R, Juneau, AK 99811. 907/465–3941 or 800/642–0066.

• Another way to see Alaska by the sea: take a voyage on a cruiseship from May to September. The cruiseships depart from Anchorage, San Francisco, and Vancouver, B.C., to sail the Inside Passage through Southeast Alaska. Itineraries vary with each ship, but common stops are Prince Rupert, Ketchikan, Juneau, Sitka, Glacier Bay, Valdez, Anchorage, Seward, Haines, Malaspina Glacier, as well as some other places. The cruise lines operating in the waters of Alaska and western Canada include Holland-America (300-AK Elliott Avenue W, Seattle, WA 98119. 206/281–0511), Princess (10100-AK, Santa Monica Boulevard, Suite 1800, Los Angeles, CA 90067. 213/553–

---

**Fire House Theater—**Cripple Creek Resort, in Ester, eight miles west via Highway 3. Shows nightly from Memorial Day to Labor Day. 907/479–2500.

**Gold Dredge No. 8—**Goldstream Road, off Highway 6 north of Fairbanks. Open 9:00 AM to 8:00 PM daily May 15 to September 15. 907/457–6058.

1770), World Explorer Cruises (555 Montgomery Street, San Francisco, CA 94111-2544. 415/391–9262 and 800/854–3835), Regency Cruises (260 Madison Avenue, New York, NY 10016. 212/972–4499) and Royal Caribbean (903 South America Way, Miami, FL 33132. 305/379–2601, 800/327–6700).

• Air travel is the best way to see some of the most incredible scenery in the world. Airlines travel between Anchorage, Fairbanks, Juneau and Ketchikan and points in Canada and the mainland United States. A much more interesting and scenic way to see Alaska is by air taxi, propeller-driven "bush planes" that land on land, ice and snow, or water. Call Wings of Alaska for flights in southeast Alaska (907/789–0790), Bush Pilots Air Service and Alaska West Air (907/776–5147) for service in the southcentral region (907/248–0149), Canning Air Service for flights in the interior and far north (907/479–3792) and the Branch River Air Service in southwest Alaska (907/246–3437 in the summer, 907/248–3539 in the winter).

• Railroads fascinate many travelers, and one of the great scenic railtrips in the world is on the Alaska Railroad, which makes the 350-mile run between Anchorage and Fairbanks, as well as routes from Anchorage to Seward and Whittier. The trains have large windows and dome cars that offer unrestricted views of the Alaska landscape. Contact Alaska Railroad, Passenger Service Department, Box 107500, Anchorage, AK 99510-7500. 800/544–0552 or 907/265–2623.

**Malemute Saloon**—Cripple Creek Resort, in Ester, eight miles west via Highway 3. "Service With a Smile," performed at 9:00 PM Monday through Saturday. 907/479–2500.

**University Museum**—907 Yukon Drive on the University of Alaska campus. Open 9:00 AM to 7:00 PM daily May through September; noon to 5:00 PM the rest of the year. 907/474–7505.

## Haines:

**Alaska Indian Arts Skill Center**—Port Chilkoot (Fort Seward). Open 9:00 AM to noon and 1:00 PM to 5:00 PM daily except Sunday, from April through October. 907/766–2610.

**Chilkat Center for the Arts**—Port Chilkoot. Indian dances on Monday, Wednesday, Thursday and Saturday evenings. 907/766–2160.

**Sheldon Museum and Cultural Center**—Main Street at the Harbor. Open 1:00 PM to 5:00 PM daily Memorial Day through early September, by appointment the rest of the year. 907/766–2236.

## Juneau:

**Alaska State Museum**—319 Whittier Street. Open 9:00 AM to 6:00 PM weekdays; 10:00 AM to 6:00 PM weekends June through September; 10:00 AM to 4:00 PM Tuesday through Saturday the rest of the year. 907/465–2901.

**City Museum**—Fourth and Main streets. Open 10:00 AM to 5:00 PM weekdays; 11:00 AM to 5:00 PM weekends during the summer. Call for winter hours. 907/586–3572.

**House of Wickersham**—213 Seventh Street. Open noon to 5:00 PM daily except Sunday, June through August, by appointment the rest of the year. 907/586–9001.

**Mendenhall Glacier Visitor Center**—Overlooks the foot of the glacier. Open 9:00 AM to 6:30 PM daily from May through September; 10:00 AM to 4:00 PM weekends in the winter. 907/789–0097.

**St. Nicholas Orthodox Church**—326 Fifth Street. Services at 7:00 PM Saturday and 10:00 AM Sunday. 907/586–1023.

## Kenai Fjords National Park:

**Park Headquarters and Visitors Center**—In Seward at the smallboat harbor. Open 8:00 AM to 7:00 PM daily in the summer; 8:00 AM to 5:00 PM daily the rest of the year. 907/224–3175.

## Ketchikan:

**Deer Mountain Fish Hatchery**—1158 Park Street. Open 9:00 AM to 12:30 PM and 1:30 PM to 5:30 PM daily. 907/225-6760.

**Dolly's House**—24 Creek Street. Open 9:00 AM to 5:00 PM daily mid-May to September or whenever cruise ships are in port. 907/225-6329.

**Saxman Native Village**—Two and an half miles south of town on S Tongass Highway. Open daily 8:00 AM to 5:00 PM; 9:00 AM to 3:00 PM holidays May 15 through September 30. 907/225-9038.

**Tongass Historical Museum**—629 Dock Street. Open 8:30 AM to 5:00 PM Monday through Saturday and 10:00 AM to 4:00 PM Sunday June through September; 1:00 PM to 5:00 PM Wednesday through Friday; 1:00 PM to 4:00 PM weekends the rest of the year. 907/225-5600.

**Totem Bight State Historical Park**—Ten miles north on the N Tongass Highway. Open daily.

## Kodiak:

**Baranov Museum**—101 Marine Way, on the harbor. Open 10:00 AM to 3:00 PM weekdays; noon to 4:00 PM weekends May through mid-September; 11:00 AM to 3:00 PM weekdays (closed Thursday) and noon to 3:00 PM Saturday the rest of the year. 907/486-5920.

**Kodiak National Wildlife Refuge**—1390 Buskin River Road. Open 8:00 AM to 4:30 PM weekdays and noon to 4:30 PM weekends. 907/487-2600.

## Sitka:

**Centennial Building**—Harbor Drive. Performances by the New Archangel Dancers when a cruise ship is in port. Call for the schedule. 907/747-5940.

**Isabelle Miller Museum**—In the Centennial Building, Harbor Drive. Open in the summer from 8:30 AM to 5:00 PM Monday through Saturday; 8:00 AM to 1:00 PM Sunday when a cruise ship is in port; 10:00 AM to 3:00 PM Tuesday through Saturday, and by appointment the rest of the year. 907/747–6455.

**St. Michael's Cathedral**—Lincoln Street. Open 11:00 AM to 3:00 PM Monday through Saturday; 11:00 AM to 3:00 PM Sunday from June to September. Services at 9:30 AM Sunday and 6:30 PM Wednesday. 907/747–8120.

**Sitka National Historical Park**—One mile east of Sitka on Lincoln Street. Visitor center open 8:00 AM to 5:00 PM daily June through September. Park grounds open year-round. 907/747–6281.

## *Skagway:*

**Arctic Brotherhood Hall**—Broadway between Second and Third Avenues. Shows from 9:00 AM to 9:00 PM daily in the summer.

**Eagles Hall**—Sixth Avenue and Broadway. Performances of "Skagway in the Days of '98" daily from mid-May to September. Gambling with fake money starts at 8:00 PM, followed by the show at 9:00 PM. 907/983–2545.

**Klondike Gold Rush National Historical Park**—In the White Pass & Yukon Route depot, Second Avenue and Broadway. Open 8:00 AM to 6:00 PM daily May through September. 907/983–2921.

**Trail of '98 Museum**—Seventh Avenue and Spring Street. Open 8:00 AM to 8:00 PM daily June through September. 907/983–2420.

**White Pass & Yukon Route**—Second Avenue and Spring Street at Broadway. Departures at 9:00 AM and 1:30 PM daily from late May to September. Fares are about $70 for adults, half that for children. 907/983–2217, 800/343–7373.

# *Romantic Retreats*

Compared to Vancouver, Victoria, Washington, and Oregon, Alaska has few elegant resorts, inns, and hotels. Accommodations range from very simple cabins to full-service modern hotels in the bigger cities. Outstanding restaurants are even more limited.

For the adventurous—travelers who are experienced backcountry explorers—the U.S. Forest Service rents a number of simple cabins in the middle of the unspoiled wilderness. There are about 200 of these cabins, which are scattered about the Tongass and Chugach National Forests. The cabins rent for $20 per night. They sleep six, and come with wood stoves, outdoor toilets, and firewood. Visitors must bring their own bedding and food. Some of the cabins are close to trails, but many require a trip by boat or plane to reach them. One other consideration is that the cabins are in bear country, and visitors should consider coming armed.

The cabins are reserved on a first-come basis, with applications taken six months in advance. The cabins are open year-round. For more information, write the U.S. Forest Service, Box 1628, Juneau, AK 99802 (907/586–8806).

Here are our favorite places to stay and dine. But first, an explanation of our cost categories:

One night in a hotel, resort, or inn for two:

*Inexpensive*—Less than $75.
*Moderate*—$75 to $125.
*Expensive*—More than $125.

Dinner for two (wine and drinks not included):

*Inexpensive*—Less than $25.
*Moderate*—$25 to $50.
*Expensive*—More than $50.

## *Romantic Lodging in Anchorage:*

**Alaska Samovar Inn**—The suites are the real jewels of this surprising hotel. The suites are quite a shock after you have seen the unimpressive standard rooms. Take the Jade Suite—all green, with a huge jacuzzi surrounded by mirrors and plants. The creativity continues in suites named the Gay '90s, the Empress, and more. Moderate. 720 Gambell Street, Anchorage, AK 99501. 907/277–1511.

**Sixth & B Bed & Breakfast**—This 1930s home, head of the Far From Fenway Fan Club (owner Peter Roberts is a Boston Red Sox fanatic) offers two double rooms that share a bath and a third floor penthouse with a private bath. Opt for the penthouse. Moderate. 145 W Sixth Avenue, Anchorage, AK 99501. 907/279–5293.

**Hotel Captain Cook**—Without a doubt the finest hotel in the state, this luxury hotel has 600 rooms located in three towers. The rooms are spacious and nicely furnished; the decor is teak and muted maroons, browns and beiges. Facilities include an athletic club, racquetball courts, indoor pool, art galleries, four restaurants, nightclub, and shopping arcade. Expensive. Fifth Avenue and K Street, Anchorage, AK 99501. 907/276–6000, 800/323–7500.

**Sheraton Anchorage Hotel**—This 407-room luxury hotel is worth visiting, if only to view the magnificent Native Alaskan art displayed in the huge lobby. The hotel has pleasant and spacious rooms. Facilities include a small health club. Expensive. 401 E Sixth Avenue, Anchorage, AK 99501. 907/276–8700, 800/325–3535.

**Voyager Hotel**—This lovely intimate hotel offers 38 mini-suites, each with a small kitchen. The rooms are beautifully decorated. Moderate. 501 K Street, Anchorage, AK 99501. 907/277–9501, 800/247–9070.

## Fine Dining in Anchorage:

**The Corsair**—Outstanding continental cuisine, with excellent beef and seafood dishes served in an intimate room. Expensive. Located in the Voyager Hotel, 501 K Street. 907/278–4502.

**Cyrano's**—This place is better for satisfying your hunger for culture than sating you with food. This bookstore offers book reviews, poetry readings, occasional concerts, and a Saturday night improv troupe (as well as sandwiches, salads, soups, espresso and capuccino, for those who find their stomachs growling). Inexpensive. 413 D Street. 907/274–2599.

**Kayak Seafood Grill**—Old photographs and caribou-horn chandeliers give this fine seafood restaurant local charm. Moderate. 510 L Street. 907/274–7617.

**Marx Bros. Cafe**—Fresh seafood and game (venison and antelope) dishes served in this 1916 house are excellent. Expensive. 627 W Third Avenue. 907/278–2133.

**Old Anchorage Salmon Bake**—Go for dinner (from 4:00 PM to 9:00 PM) when this restaurant in a series of tents offers a feast with salmon, halibut, crab, reindeer, and more. Moderate. Third Avenue and K Street. 907/279–8790.

**Tundra Club**—Authenic native cuisine—Indian fry bread, berry dumplings, reindeer sausage, fish pie, and sourdough pancakes. The dishes are all excellent, even if they aren't for the weight-conscious. Moderate. 250 Gambell Street. 907/278–4716.

## Romantic Lodging in Fairbanks:

**Captain Bartlett Inn**—Old Alaska is the theme here, with totem poles outside the front entrance, spruce log walls covered with Alaska momentos, and photographs—this hotel has the true feel of a hunting lodge. The 198 rooms are simple but comfortable. Moderate. 1411 Airport Way, Fairbanks, AK 99701. 907/452–1888, 800/544–7528, 800/478–7900 in Alaska.

**Westmark Fairbanks**—The best hotel in town, this sprawling hotel offers 240 large and tastefully decorated rooms. The Westmark Fairbanks is owned by Westours, which means that most guests will be part of large groups. Expensive. 820 Noble Street, Fairbanks, AK 99701. 907/456–7722, 800/544–0970.

For B&Bs, contact Fairbanks Bed & Breakfast for a list of available rooms. Most of the rooms are in private homes and are comfortable and inexpensive. Fairbanks Bed & Breakfast, P.O. Box 74573, Fairbanks, AK 99707. 907/452–4967.

## Fine Dining in Fairbanks:

**Cafe de Paris**—Excellent quiches, croissant sandwiches, crepes, soups, and salads. Inexpensive. 801 Pioneer Road. 907/456–1669.

**Gambardello's**—Art Deco meets Italian chef in the elegant dining room where the best dishes are seafood and pasta combinations. Moderate. 706 Second Avenue. 907/456-3417.

**Pump House**—Located in a pump house once used to pump water to a gold-dredging operation, this old building offers fine continental dishes, a superb oyster bar (with entertainment Thursday through Sunday nights), and numerous relics from its gold-mining days. Members of the Fairbanks Symphony perform at Sunday brunch. Moderate. At milepost 1.3 on the Chena Pump Road. 907/479-8452.

## Romantic Lodging in Haines:

**Hotel Halsingland**—Located in the old top officers' quarters at the former Fort Seward, this hotel offers 60 individually decorated and comfortable rooms and a lot of ambience. The hotel is near the Alaska Indian Art Skills Center and the Chilkat Center for the Arts. Inexpensive. P.O. Box 158, Haines, AK 99827. 907/766-2000, 800/542-6363, 800/478-2525 in Alaska.

**Fort Seward Bed & Breakfast**—Located in a renovated 1904 Victorian that served as the chief surgeon's quarters at Fort Seward, this B&B has three spacious and comfortable guest rooms. Moderate. No. 1 Officers Row, P.O. Box 5, Haines, AK 99827. 907/766-2856.

## Fine Dining in Haines:

**Commander's Room**—Located in the Hotel Halsingland, this dining room features excellent seafood and beef. Moderate. 907/766-2000.

**Port Chilkoot Potlach**—This all-you-can-eat salmon bake is at the Tribal House on the Fort Seward parade grounds. The bake, run by the Hotel Halsingland, is offered from 5:00 PM to 8:00 PM each evening during the summer. Inexpensive. 907/766-2000.

**The Catalyst**—A European-style cafe featuring excellent seafood, quiches, soups, and a salad bar. Inexpensive. Main Street between Third and Fourth. 907/766-2670.

## Romantic Lodging in Juneau:

**Alaska Hotel & Bar**—The bar—really an elegant lounge furnished with stained wood, brass trim, and stained glass—is where the elite meet, and the hotel is a Victorian delight. There are 40 rooms, each decorated in what some call bordello style—antique beds, dresser, sink and toilets (some rooms share baths), and red and blue drapes and carpeting. Inexpensive. 167 S Franklin Street, Juneau, AK 99801. 907/586-1000, 800/327-9347.

**Inn at the Waterfront**—This former nineteenth-century bordello opposite the cruise ship terminal has been converted into a 21-room inn, featuring antique furnishings. Inexpensive. 455 S Franklin Street, Juneau, AK 99801. 907/586-2050.

**Prospector Hotel**—The rooms are enormous at this pleasant hotel next to the state museum. Moderate. 375 Whittier Street, Juneau, AK 99801. 907/586-3737, 800/331-2711.

**Westmark-Baranof Hotel**—This majestic 50-year-old hotel has 202 rooms, efficiencies, and suites, each spacious and comfortable. The hotel is convenient to all downtown attractions. Don't miss the oil paintings in the lobby done by Alaskan artists, or the fine pianist in the bar. Moderate. 127 N Franklin Street, Juneau, AK 99801. 907/586-2660, 800/544-0970.

**Westmark Juneau**—This seven-story highrise offers 105 modern and spacious rooms across from the docks. Expensive. 51 W Egan Drive, Juneau, AK 99801. 907/586-6900, 800/544-0970.

## Fine Dining in Juneau:

**The Cook House**—Don't say you weren't warned. In the back corner is a scaffold, noose and a sign declaring: "The cooking has never killed anyone, but the miners have hung more than one cook." Actually, the fare here—giant burgers, slab-sized steaks, excellent seafood—is fairly good. We don't think they have hanged any cooks recently. Moderate. 200 Admiral Bay. 907/463-3658.

**The Fiddlehead**—Tired of salmon and steaks? Visit this attractive restaurant, which features pasta and rice dishes. The chicken and sauteed eggplant is excellent. Inexpensive. 429 Willoughby Avenue. 907/586-3150.

**Gold Creek Salmon Bake**—All-you-can-eat, as long as you want alder-smoked salmon, salad, and trimmings. This cookout is at the end of Basin Street on the banks of Gold Creek, near where Juneau and Harris made their first strike. Moderate. 907/586-1424.

**Luna's**—The best Italian restaurant in town. Okay, there isn't much competition, but Luna's is quite good, featuring great pastas and seafood combinations, as well as good veal, chicken, and steaks. Moderate. 210 Seward Street. 907/586-6990.

**New Orpheum Cafe**—This '60s-style coffee house is a good place to have a slice of quiche, dessert, or an espresso. Added attractions are the art exhibits and classical music concerts. Inexpensive. 245 Marine Way. 907/463-5655.

**Silverbow Inn**—Innovative cuisine—rosemary lamb chops, salmon Florentine—that is a delightful change from all the seafood-and-beef places. Dinner is by candlelight in a room furnished with antiques. Moderate. 120 Second Street. 907/586-4146.

**Thane Ore House**—All-you-can-eat, with salmon, halibut, and barbecued ribs on the menu. This feast is in a recreated nineteenth-century miners' mess hall. Try your hand at panning for gold between courses. Inexpensive. 4400 Thane Road. 907/586-3442.

## Romantic Lodging in Ketchikan:

**Royal Executive Suites**—This small luxury hotel built on pilings over the Tongass Narrows offers 14 pleasant rooms and six spacious suites (all with complete kitchens). Expensive. 1471 Tongass Avenue, P. O. Box 8331, Ketchikan, AK 99901. 907/225-1900.

**Salmon Falls Resort**—This luxury waterfront fishing resort has 36 rooms located in rustic-looking lodges. The rooms are luxurious, though, and the resort offers everything for the angler. Expensive. Mile 17 N Tongas Highway, Ketchikan, AK 99901. 907/225-2752, 800/247-9059.

**Westmark Cape Fox Lodge**—You have to ride an inclined railroad up to this lodge, which overlooks downtown Ketchikan and the waterfront. The lodge offers 72 spacious and comfortable rooms. Moderate. 800 Ventia Way, Ketchikan, AK 99901. 907/ 225–8001, 800/544–0970 in the U.S., 800/999–2570 in Canada.

## Fine Dining in Ketchikan:

**Charley's**—First-rate seafood served in a clublike room with lots of brass and dark wood. Moderate. 208 Front Street. 907/ 225–5090.

**Gilmore Garden**—The menu is ambitious by Alaskan standards—entrecote marchand de vin, pollo alla cacciatora, for example—but the results are excellent. The dining room is attractively decorated with numerous plants and rattan pieces. Moderate. In the Gilmore Hotel, 326 Front Street. 907/225– 9423.

**Salmon Falls Resort**—Excellent seafood and steaks served at this fine resort's dining room. Expensive. Mile 17 N Tongass Highway. 907/225–2752, 800/247–9059.

## Romantic Lodging in Kodiak:

**Kodiak Buskin River Inn**—Closer to the airport than town, this modern hotel has 51 comfortable rooms and six spacious suites. Moderate. 1395 Airport Way, P.O. Box 89, Kodiak, AK 99615. 907/487–2700.

**Westmark Kodiak**—This downtown hotel offers 89 comfortable rooms. Moderate. 236 S Rezanof Drive, P.O. Box 1547, Kodiak, AK 99615. 907/486–5712.

## Fine Dining in Kodiak:

**Chart Room**—Located in the Westmark Kodiak Hotel, this seafood-and-steak dining room is the best in town. Moderate. 236 S Rezanof Drive. 907/486–5712.

**El Chicano**—Great Mexican food, particularly the chicken mole. Inexpensive. 104 Center Avenue. 907/486–6116.

## Romantic Lodging in Seward (for Kenai Fjords Park):

**New Seward Hotel**—This charming hotel offers 58 comfortable rooms and all sorts of courtesies (van rides to the harbor, ferry, and train station, coffee in the lobby, first-name service, and other delights). Moderate. 217 Fifth Avenue, P.O. Box 675, Seward, AK 99664. 907/224–8001.

**Van Gilder Hotel**—This 1909 landmark, Seward's oldest building, has been renovated and now offers 26 pleasant rooms furnished with European antiques. Moderate. 308 Adams Street, P.O. Box 775, Seward, AK 99664. 907/224–3079.

## Fine Dining in Seward:

**Harbor Dinner Club**—The decor and menu are nautical; the daily specials are the best on the menu. Moderate. 220 Fifth Avenue. 907/224–3012.

## Romantic Lodging in Sitka:

**Karras B&B**—Five pleasant rooms in a friendly and cozy B&B close to downtown make this place a real find. Inexpensive. 230 Kogwanton Street, Sitka, AK 99835. 907/747–3978.

**Westmark Shee Atika**—Even if you aren't a guest, stop by to see the Native Alaskan art throughout the hotel. And if you are staying in one of the 96 spacious rooms, the artwork is an added delight. Moderate. 330 Seward Street, P.O. Box 78, Sitka, AK 99835. 907/747–6241, 800/544–0970.

## Fine Dining in Sitka:

**Channel Club**—Winner of several gourmet awards, this restaurant features the finest steaks and the freshest seafood in town—whatever you choose, you cannot make a mistake. Moderate. Milepost 3.5 on the Halibut Point Road. 907/747–9916.

**Marina Restaurant**—Seafood is featured here but the Mexican and Italian dishes are good, too. Moderate. 205 Harbor Drive (second floor). 907/747–8840.

**Raven Room**—The native artwork that fills this beautiful dining room is excellent, a fitting match for the fine seafood, steaks, and pasta. Moderate. In the Westmark Shee Atika Hotel, 330 Seward Street. 907/747-6241.

## Romantic Lodging in Skagway:

**The Skagway Inn**—This cozy inn (once a boarding house for women) offers 14 pleasant rooms, each named after a woman who stayed here in the 1890s and each furnished differently with period antiques. Inexpensive. Broadway near Seventh Avenue. P.O. Box 500, Skagway, AK 99840. 907/983-2289.

**Westmark Inn**—The best hotel in town (if you can stomach the Gay '90s/Gold Rush decor and the prospect of spending a night surrounded by tour groups). The 100 and 200 series rooms have the Gay '90s decor. There are 220 rooms in all, comfortable and well-equipped. The hotel is open from mid-May to September 30. Expensive. Third Avenue, between Spring Street and Broadway. P.O. Box 515, Skagway, AK 99840. 907/983-2291.

**Wind Valley Lodge**—This pleasant lodge, located a mile north of town, offers 30 spacious rooms, each nicely furnished. Inexpensive. P.O. Box 354, Skagway, AK 99840. 907/983-2236.

## Fine Dining in Skagway:

**Chilkoot Dining Room**—The salmon cooked with brown sugar and the apple-almond chicken are the stars of the menu at this fine restaurant in the Westmark Inn. Moderate. Third Avenue between Spring Street and Broadway. 907/983-2291.

**Prospector's Sourdough Restaurant**—Excellent salmon and steaks. Inexpensive. On Broadway between Fourth and Fifth Streets. 907/983-2865.

Horseback riding in the Alberta mountains is a popular attraction. *(Photograph courtesy Alberta Tourism)*

CHAPTER 7

# *Wilderness Adventures and Lodges*

*C*hallenging adventures and wilderness experiences await you in the wild and wonderful Pacific Northwest. Here you can take a raft or jet boat through the white water of dangerous rivers, or cast a fly for trout and troll for salmon that often top 50 pounds.

The Northwest's many mountains offer a wide variety of adventures. In summer, you can hike the mountains' trails, climb their summits, and bicycle through their slopes. In winter, a wide variety of outdoor experiences await, from downhill skiing to dogsled expeditions through the frozen wilderness.

There are hundreds of groups organizing such wilderness adventures. Here is a sampling of the resorts, lodges, and outfitters that can help you experience the adventure of your dreams. (For a more comprehensive list, contact the state tourism authority. The cost factor here varies widely. We suggest you contact the lodge, resort, or outfitter directly for current rates.)

## *Riding the Wild Rivers*

Lara House is a fine inn offering four pleasant rooms in a 1910 home, as well as serving as a base of white water trips in central Oregon. Lara House is owned by Cheryl Hukari, who also operates a white water rafting outfitter. Hukari can organize any type of river ride, from a half-day gentle float or a day-long ride through some challenging rapids to multi-night trips on the lower Deschutes Rivers. 640 NW Congress, Bend, OR 97701. 503/388–4064.

Here are some other choices:

### *Alaska:*

**Alaska Discovery Inc.**—This outfitter organizes 11-day trips on the Alsek and Tatshenshini rivers from the inland mountains to the Gulf of Alaska. P.O. Box 26, Gustavus, AK 99826. 907/697–2257.

**Sourdough Outfitters**—Raft, kayak, and canoe trips through the wild rivers of the Brooks Range. Pass through Class I and II water and see incredible landscape and wildlife. Box 18-AT, Bettles, AK 99726. 907/692–5252.

## Alberta:

**WB Adventures Ltd.**—One and two-day river rafting trips on the Upper Red Deer River near Calgary, with overnight stays in cabins. Box 3398, Station B, Calgary, AB T2M 4M1. 403/637–2060.

**Whitewater Rafting Ltd.**—Two, three and four-hour white-water rafting trips on the Maligne or Sunwapta rivers near Jasper. Box 362, Jasper, AB T0E 1E0. 403/852–4721.

## British Columbia:

**Frontier River Adventures**—One and two-day trips on the white waters of the Thompson and Fraser Rivers. 927 Fairfield Road, North Vancouver, BC V7H 2J4. 604/929–7612.

## Oregon:

**Hells Canyon Adventures**—Two-hour and all-day jet-boat tours on the Snake River, with runs on Class IV rapids and stops at ancient Indian villages and pioneer homesteads. P.O. Box 159, Oxbrow, OR 97840. 503/785–3352, 800/HCA-FLOAT in Oregon.

**Jerry's Rogue River Jet Boats**—See wildlife, pioneer homesteads, and other scenic delights in this 60-mile round-trip run up the Rogue River. Box 1011, Gold Beach, OR 97444. 503/247–7601.

**Oregon Guides and Packers**—Clearing house for professional guides offering raft or jet-boat trips on the McKenzie, Rogue, and other Oregon rivers. Box 10841, Eugene, OR 97440. 503/683–9552.

# Canoeing and Kayaking

**Sundance Expeditions, Inc.** has long been called the College of Kayaking, for its excellent classes and helpful instructors. Sundance offers nine night courses in kayaking. The first five days are spent in a base camp, with classes in the daytime and nights in a comfy lodge; the last four days of the course are spent traveling the river. 14894 Galice Road, Merlin, OR 97532. 503/479-8508.

Other choices:

## Alaska:

**Alaska Discovery Expeditions**—Four to ten-day kayak and canoe trips throughout Alaska. 369-AK S Franklin Street, Juneau, AK 99801. 907/586-1911.

## Alberta:

**Tomahawk Canoe Trips**—Half-day to week-long trips in the Rocky Mountain foothills near Jasper National Park. 11035 64 Avenue, Edmonton, AB T6H 1T4. 403/436-9189.

## British Columbia:

**Tofino Sea Kayaking Co.**—Paddles up the fjords of Clayoquot Sound on Vancouver Island. 320 Main Street, Tofino, BC V0R 2Z0. 604/725-4222.

## Oregon:

**Sunrise Scenic Tours**—Courses and tours on the Deschutes, Klamath, Illinois, and Rogue rivers. The kayak trips last from one to five days. 3791 Rogue River Highway, Gold Hill, OR 97525. 503/582-0202.

## Washington:

**Liberty Bell Alpine Tours**—One-day introductory clinics to white water canoeing. Mazama, WA 98833. 509/996-2250.

# *Fantastic Fishing*

The Pacific Northwest is an angler's paradise. One of the finest destinations for the sport is the April Point Lodge on Vancouver Island. Considered by many to be the finest fishing lodge in the region, April Point tries hard to live up to that claim. The 38-room lodge is first class in every way: it has 65 Boston whalers for guests to use for fishing, 45 experts to guide them through the waters, luxury accommodations ranging from studio apartments and lodge rooms to multibedroom guest houses, and a highly praised restaurant. It's almost too luxurious to be thought of as only a fishing lodge. P.O. Box 1, Campbell River, BC V9W 4Z9. 604/285-3329.

Here are a few of the best of the fishing lodges in the region:

## *Alaska:*

**Alaska Sportfishing Lodge Association—**This group represents thirty of the state's top fishing lodges. Contact them for details about all of the resorts. 800/352-2003.

## *Alberta:*

**Christina Lake Lodge—**Fish for northern pike, walleye, and arctic grayling on Christina Lake. Guests stay in 16 rooms in the lodge or in eight fully equipped cabins. c/o General Delivery, Conklin, AB T0P 1H0. 403/559-2224.

## *British Columbia:*

**Corbett Lake Country Inn—**This log cabin is a three-hour drive east of Vancouver, on two lakes filled with trout. Only fly-fishing is allowed on the lakes. If you fail to catch dinner, don't despair. The lodge is just as famous for its grand continental restaurant as it is for its excellent fishing. Guests stay in three rooms in the lodges or ten spacious cabins. Box 327, Merritt, BC V0K 2B0. 604/378-4334.

**Painter's Lodge—**This 70-room hotel replaced the original rustic lodge, which was destroyed by fire in 1985. It offers contemporary and comfortable accommodations, a fine restaurant, and great salmon fishing in the Quinsam and Campbell rivers. Guides are available to help you find the big ones. 1625 MacDonald Road, Campbell River, BC V9W 4S5. 604/286–1102, 800/663–7090 in Canada.

### Oregon:

**House on the Metolius**—The Metolius River is a perfect trout stream, and this inn on the banks of the river in central Oregon offers eight rooms in cabins on a cliff overlooking the river. FS Road 1420, P.O. Box 601, Camp Sherman, OR 97730. 503/595–6620.

**Steamboat Inn**—This outstanding resort is on the North Umpqua River, nearly in the center of the stretch of white water famous for its steelhead trout. Accommodations are in four rustic duplex cabins, which are simple but comfortable, and five newer, two-level cottages. Steamboat Inn is also famous for its fine restaurant, which serves a fantastic Fisherman's Dinner featuring the finest and freshest in seafood, meats, pastas, and vegetables. Steamboat, OR 97447–9703. 503/498–2411.

### Washington:

**Olson's Charters**—Located on the extreme northwestern tip of the Olympic Peninsula, this charter service makes trips in pursuit of giant salmon and halibut. Box 216, Sekiv, WA 98381. 206/963–2311.

# Climb Every Mountain

Here is a list of outfitters:

### Alaska:

**Mountain Trip**—Expeditions to and seminars about the highest mountains in Alaska. Box 41161, Dept. AT, Anchorage, AK 99509. 907/345–6499.

## Alberta:

**Banff Alpine Guides**—Personalized class and climbing expeditions in the mountains of western Canada. Box 1025, Banff, AB T0L 0C0. 403/678-6091.

## British Columbia:

**Kootenai Wilderness Recreation**—Customized mountain-climbing trips for one to four climbers. Argenta, BC V0G 1B0. 604/366-4480.

## Oregon:

**Timberline Mountain Guides**—Half-day to five-day courses covering all skill levels. Climbs are guided year-round in the Oregon mountains. P.O. Box 464-C, Terrebonne, OR 97760. 503/548-1888.

## Washington:

**American Alpine Institute**—Classes and guided climbs for all skill levels, with most courses in the northern Cascades of Washington. 1212 24th D, Bellingham, WA 98225. 206/671-1505.

**Liberty Bell Alpine Tours**—These outfitters offer beginners five-day seminars that end with a major climb, operating from a camp in the Cascades. Mazama, WA 98833. 509/996-2250.

**Rainier Mountaineering**—One-day classes, guided climbs, and longer seminars, from May to September. Paradise, WA 98397. 206/627-6242 September through May, 206/569-2227 June through August.

# Dogsled Tours

The best way to see the landscape and wildlife of Denali National Park and Preserve is by dogsled. You can experience this unique form of travel with Denali Dog Tours, which offers customized trips through the national park. Stays are in log cabins (or wall tents heated by wood stoves). Trips are offered November through April. Box 670, Denali NP, AK 99755. 907/683–2644.

Here is a list of other dogsled outfitters:

## Alaska:

**Brooks Range Wilderness Trips**—Week-long sled trips, with nights in lodges. Good physical condition required. P.O. Box 40, Bettles, AK 99726. 907/692–5312.

## Oregon:

**Wilderness Freighters**—Two to four-day trips in the Mt. Adams foothills, with overnight stops in huts. 2166 SE 142nd Avenue, Portland, OR 97233. 503/761–7428.

# Bicycle Tours

Here is a list of outfitters who can help you organize a trip:

## Alaska:

**Backroads Bicycle Touring**—Eight-day inn tours from Anchorage to Prince William Sound, with return by rail. Average daily mileage is 50 or more miles. These trips are offered in July, August, and September. 1516 Fifth Street, Berkeley, CA 94710–1713. 415/527–1555, 800/533–2573.

## Alberta:

**Rocky Mountain Cycle Tours**—This outfitter offers six-night tours, starting and ending in Banff. Overnight stops are in rustic cabins and inns. The riders cover an average of 20 miles a day. A camping/lodge tour is available, though the daily mileage is 40 miles. Box 895-A, Banff, AB T0L 0C0. 403/678–6770.

## British Columbia:

**Backroads Bicycle Touring**—Five-day inn tours of the Gulf Islands. Average daily mileage is 30 to 35 miles. These trips are offered in June, July, and September. 1516 Fifth Street, Berkeley, CA 94710–1713. 415/527–1555, 800/533–2573.

## Oregon:

**Backroads Bicycle Touring**—Five-day inn or camping tours of Oregon's forests west of Portland. Average daily mileage is 50+ miles. These trips are offered in June, July, and September. 1516 Fifth Street, Berkeley, CA 94710–1713. 415/527–1555, 800/533–2573.

## Washington:

**Backroads Bicycle Touring**—Six-day inn or camping tours of the San Juan Islands. Average daily mileage is 40 miles. These trips are offered in July and August. 1516 Fifth Street, Berkeley, CA 94710–1713. 415/527–1555, 800/533–2573.

**Liberty Bell Alpine Tours**—Three to five-day cycling tours in the San Juan Islands or the Cascades. Nights are spent at country inns. Mazama, WA 98833. 509/966–2250.

# Pack Trips by Horse

Experience life on the range by taking a multiday trip by horse. One such outfitter offering horsepack trips is Lute Jerstad Adventures of Portland, Oregon. This outfitter organizes three to five-day adventures that start at a rustic mountain cabin and then head up more than 8,000 feet into the Wallowa Mountains. By night you camp under the stars next to crystal-clear lakes. It's great for fishing, sighting rare and endangered wildlife (bighorn sheep, cougar, wolves, etc.), or just traveling in some of the most scenic land you will ever see. P.O. Box 19537, Portland, OR 97219. 503/244–4364.

Here is a list of other outfitters who can help you organize a trip:

## Alaska:

**Kachemak Bay Horse Trips**—One to four-day trips, with overnights at historic ranches on the eastern shore of the Kenai Peninsula. P.O. Box 2004, Homer, AK 99603. 907/235–7850.

## Alberta:

**Amethyst Lakes Pack Trips**—Located in the Tonquin Valley of Jasper National Park, this outfitter organizes rides from a serene cabin camp. Guests stay in the cabins and ride, fish, hike, or explore during the day. Box 508, Jasper, AB T0E 1E0. 403/866–3980 June through September, 403/865–4417 October through May.

## British Columbia:

**Headwaters Outfitting Ltd.**—Trips for small parties into Jasper National Park and other wilderness areas. Riders stay in base camps. P.O. Box 818, Valemount, BC V0E 2Z0. 604/566–4718.

## Oregon:

**Cal Henry**—Horseback trips in eastern Oregon range from simple overnight rides to longer explorations of the Hells Canyon National Recreation Area. Box 26-A, Joseph, OR 97846. 503/432–9171.

## Washington:

**Sun Mountain Lodge**—You can take a trail ride to breakfast or join a longer pack trip at this lodge in the Cascades. Recently remodeled, this inn also offers a heated pool, tennis courts, hot tub, and stunning views of the Methow Valley. The best rooms are the newest: each has a fireplace and great view of the valley. Expensive. Patterson Lake Road, nine miles south of Winthrop. P.O. Box 1000, Winthrop, WA 98862. 509/996–2211.

# Ski Touring

The snow-covered wilderness is even more interesting when you leave the crowded trails and roads and enter the serene world of the backcountry on your nordic skis. Alaska Discovery conducts cross-country ski trips on the Juneau ice fields. The six-day trips include first-rate ski and glacier travel gear, daily instruction and practice, and a 40-pound pack of supplies. It isn't for beginners, but it is an exceptional adventure. P.O. Box 26, Gustavus, AK 99826. 907/697–2257.

Here is a list of other outfitters:

## Alaska:

**Denali Dog Tours**—Custom ski trips to any destination inside the Denali National Park, with overnight stays in heated cabins. Box 670, Denali NP, AK 99755. 907/683–2644.

## Alberta:

**Skoki Lodge**—This rugged lodge located more than seven miles from a road and 7,200 feet up offers magnificent skiing on backcountry trails. The overnight trips are in Banff National Park. Box 5, Lake Louise, AB T0L 1E0. 403/522–3555.

## British Columbia:

**Chute Lake Resort**—This rustic six-cabin resort in the Okanagan Mountains offers great cross-country skiing, snowmobiling, ice-fishing, and other winter activities. The cabins are simple but comfortable, the dining room adequate. Call for directions. c/o 797 Alexander Avenue, Penticton, BC V2A 1E6. 604/493–3535.

## Oregon:

**Elk Lake Resort**—This remote 12-cabin resort is on Elk Lake, reachable only by ten miles of skiing or on a snowmobile in the winter. The skiing is great, much better than the simple but comfortable cabins and adequate restaurant. Write for more information; Elk Lake Lodge doesn't have a phone. P.O. Box 789, Bend, OR 97709.

## Washington:

**Liberty Bell Alpine Tours**—Take a helicopter from the Mazama Country Inn into the northern Cascades and then take a gentle, all-day ski tour back to the lodge. Mazama, WA 98833. 509/966–2250.

## Naturalist Expeditions

A number of groups offer educational trips that focus on the animals, plants, geology, and history of the region. The subject of the trips varies each year, so contact these groups directly for the current schedule of trips:

♠ **Audubon Naturalist Society**—8940 Jones Mill Road, Chevy Chase, MD. 20815. 301/652–5964. ext. 3006.

♠ **Ecosummer Expeditions**—1516 Duranleau Street, Vancouver, BC V6H 3S4. 604/669–7741

♠ **Mountain Travel**—1398-AG, Solano Avenue, Albany, CA 94706. 800/227–2384, 415/527–8100.

♠ **Nature Expeditions International**—474 Willamette Avenue, Box 11496, Dept. AGN, Eugene, OR 97440. 503/484–6529.

♠ **Questers Worldwide Nature Tours**—257 Park Avenue S, New York, NY 10010. 800/468–8668.

♠ **The Resource Institute**—6532 Phinney Avenue N, Building B, Seattle, WA 98103. 206/784–6762.

♠ **Special Odysseys**—P.O. Box 37, Medina, WA 98039. 206/455–1960.

♠ **Smithsonian Odyssey Tours**—Contact Saga International Holidays Ltd., 120 Boylston Street, Boston, MA 02116. 800/258–5885.

The venerable Empress Hotel in Victoria, B.C., where Christmas and New Year's are celebrated in style. *(Leone & Leone Ltd.)*

CHAPTER **8**

# *Murder Mystery and More*

🌲　🌲　🌲　🌲　🌲　🌲　🌲　🌲

*T*he Murder Capital of the Northwest isn't found on the mean streets of some big city. No, the center of mayhem in the Pacific Northwest is in a little village on a quiet, rural island.

That village is Langley, on Whidbey Island in Puget Sound. At the end of February or beginning of March each year, Langley holds a Murder Mystery Weekend. Townfolks taking roles as actors stage the mystery, based on a script written by a different author each year. Sleuths get background information on the crime from the Chamber of Commerce, and then can visit the scene of the crime and search for clues in the town's shops.

The Murder Mystery events start Saturday morning and continue through Sunday evening. Many participants come dressed for their part as investigators.

It's great fun and inexpensive; the Chamber of Commerce requests donations to defray costs. Sleuths often stay in the many fine inns and hotels on the island during their search for justice. For more information, contact the Langley Chamber of Commerce, 124 1/2 Second Street, Langley, WA 98260. 206/321–6765.

The Langley Murder Mystery Weekend is one of several offbeat getaways in the Northwest. You can help solve a crime, take a class in painting, pamper yourself at a spa, saddle up at a dude or real working ranch, or spend a weekend on a large boat. Here's a guide to some different getaways:

Package rates are broken down this way: lodging (and activities) for two people for one night:

*Inexpensive*—Less than $100.
*Moderate*—$100 to $150.
*Expensive*—$200 and more.

We will mention whether all or some meals are included in the package.

## Playing Detective

**Fort Worden Park**—This decommissioned fort on the tiny finger of land at Port Townsend is now a state park. The ten Victorian houses used as lodging for the officers are now open to guests who want to get involved in a little sleuthing. The homes are very large (some five bedrooms) and are furnished with Victorian era pieces. Guest detectives on Murder Mystery Weekends work as teams. The murder is the work of Murder by Invitation, a professional acting troupe. The mystery weekend is offered in either the spring or the fall. The two-night package is expensive, and includes all meals. Contact Murder by Invitation, P.O. Box 1201, Port Towsend, WA 98368. 206/385–6116.

**Old Mill House Bed and Breakfast**—It's a perfect setting for nefarious doings: a 1920s lumber baron's mansion big enough to hold a speakeasy, dance floor, and monthly jam sessions. Now an elegant B&B, this inn holds Murder Mystery Weekends every six to eight weeks from November to May. There are three attractive rooms (named after Bessie Smith, F. Scott Fitzgerald, and Will Rogers) and one stunning suite: the Isadora Duncan Suite, a lavish mauve, green, and gray delight. If you have an itch to write, put your pen to the novel-in-progress in the Fitzgerald room. The murder mystery usually has a theme (1890s, circus, 1920s gangsters), a script, actors, and roles for the guest detectives (the inn has a lot of vintage clothing for last-minute costumes). Each mystery weekend includes a one night stay. Inexpensive, Sunday brunch included. 116 Oak Street, P.O. Box 543, Eatonville, WA 98328. 206/832–6506.

**Outlook Inn**—Murder by Invitation brings its actors, script, and victims to this Orcas Island inn, a 30-room white clapboard structure. The Murder Mystery, offered once every October, is similar to that held at Fort Worden Park. The two-night package is expensive and includes all meals. Contact Murder by Invitation, P.O. Box 1201, Port Towsend, WA 98368. 206/385–6116.

**Qualicum College Inn**—The former private boys school in British Columbia is located in a Tudor Manor, an appropriate setting for murder. The 70 rooms are furnished in a variety of styles, from standard and unexciting furnishings to contemporary and lovely pieces. The best rooms, recently renovated, are furnished with pine furniture and Laura Ashley fabrics. Some rooms have fireplaces and some have mountain or ocean views. The Murder Mystery Weekends, produced by a professional cast of actors, occur four or five times a year. The package includes a Friday night reception, two breakfasts, one dinner, and Sunday Brunch. Expensive. The inn is a two-hour drive north of Victoria, B.C. P.O. Box 99, Qualicum Beach, BC V0R 2T0. 604/752–9262, 800/663–7306.

**Winchester Country Inn**—This handsome century-old Victorian inn was completely renovated in 1983. It now offers seven attractive guest rooms, all furnished with period pieces. The inn holds two Murder Mystery Weekends each month from November through March, as well as a handful of Scavenger Hunt Weekends. The two-night packages include two breakfasts, two five-course dinners, and two champagne parties. Moderate. 35 S Second Street, Ashland, OR 97520. 503/488–1113.

## *Play Out Your Fantasies*

**Fantasyland Hotel**—Even if the location isn't itself a bit of a fantasyland (the massive West Edmonton Mall), this luxury hotel offers 360 rooms, 240 of which we can ignore for the moment. The other 120 "themed" rooms are what we find very interesting. You can stay in the Roman Room, where white marble sculptures, a round red velvet bed with silk draperies, and an authentic Roman bath may give you some new perspectives on history. Or you can spend some time in the Polynesian Room, with its floating warrior catamaran, waterfall cascading into a rock pool, and an optional erupting volcano. (We are not making this up!) The Victorian Coach Room offers a bed set in an elegant coach from the era; the Hollywood Room features lots of neon, a carpet with lights, and a sybaritic black-tiled spa. For more rural tastes, the Truck Room has a bed located in a renovated truck that gives new meaning to the term "pickup." In between bouts of fantasy, you can stroll into the West Edmonton Mall, a setting of 800 shops, an amusement park, a roller coaster, and more, which helps put these "Fantasy Theme Rooms" into perspective. Call for your favorite fantasy, many of which are booked weeks in advance. Expensive. 17700 87 Avenue, Edmonton, AB T5T 4V4. 403/444–3000, 800/661–6454 in Canada.

# Art Workshops

**Flying L Ranch**—This 160-acre ranch near Mt. Adams in Washington state is an unlikely setting for autumn workshops on watercolors, oil painting, and other art media. There are six pleasant rooms in the huge lodge, five more in a guest house plus two single-party cottages. The rooms are decorated with a mélange of cheery country furnishings and original western art. The three-day weekends are expensive and include meals. Call for directions. 25 Flying L Lane, Glenwood, WA 98619. 509/364–3488.

# Life in the Old West

**Flying U Guest Ranch**—Take a hayride, kick up your heels at a square dance, or just hang around the saloon at this 25,000-acre working ranch, which raises Texas longhorns and cattle. Participate in a roundup, ride the trails, go canoeing or fishing, or save your energy for the twice-weekly dances. Guests stay in 25 rustic but comfortable rooms. Moderate, meals included. Box 69, 70 Mile House, BC V0K 2K0. 604/456–7717.

**Green Springs Box R Ranch**—There are 50 covered wagons, a stagecoach, a buckboard, and a buggy on this cattle ranch. Other attractions include an old pioneer town, the wagon ruts made by the emigrants on the Applegate Trail, a boot hill, and a surprisingly good museum featuring pioneer and Indian artifacts. Guests stay in four fully equipped log or cedar houses. Inexpensive, but you will have to bring your own food. The ranch is 25 miles from Ashland. 16799 Highway 66, Ashland, OR 97520. 503/482–1873.

**Homeplace Guest Ranch**—You can ride on the trails or take an overnight horseback trip at this ranch, which was first homesteaded in the early 1900s. Guests stay in rooms in the main ranch house. Other activities include hiking, fishing, sleigh rides, cross-country skiing, or just soothing those saddle sores in a hot tub. Moderate, all meals included. Site 2, Box 66, RR1, Priddies, AB T0L 1W0. 403/931–3245.

**Sundance Ranch**—You can relive (if only a little bit) the exciting scene from "Dances With Wolves" by saddling up one of the one hundred horses at this British Columbia dude ranch and riding out to the fields to see the small herd of buffalo that live here. In the spring, if you dare, you can participate in branding and the cattle roundup. There are 31 attractive pine-paneled rooms in the annexes to the main house. Moderate, all meals included. The ranch is about a four hour drive from Vancouver. Box 489, Ashcroft, BC V0K 1A0. 604/453–2422.

## The Spa Life

**Carson Hot Mineral Springs Resort**—Located on the Washington side of the Columbia River Gorge, this 1897 resort hotel offers hot mineral baths and massages. The resort has two white frame buildings—one is the hotel and dining room, the other is the bathhouse—and 13 cabins. Accommodations are simple. Inexpensive. Windriver Highway two miles from Highway 14. P.O. Box 370, Carson, WA 98610. 509/427–8292.

**Harrison Hot Springs Resort**—The original building dates to the 1920s at this 340-room spa east of Vancouver, B.C. The attractions include the thermal springs, lovely grounds, tennis courts, exercise circuit, indoor pools (103 and 90 degrees), outdoor pool (90 degrees), and lake cruises. The drawbacks: the rooms need renovating, which was being planned at this writing, and the food is average. Expensive. 100 Esplanade Avenue, Harrison Hot Springs, BC V0M 1K0, 604/796–2244.

**108 Hills Health & Guest Ranch**—This British Columbia resort offers coed health and conditioning programs featuring aerobics, dancefit, aquafit, massage, and powerwalking, as well as classes in beauty and makeup. It's not all work and workouts, though. The resort offers hayrides, barn dancing, tepee parties, and other fun-filled diversions. The spa accepts about two dozen guests at a time. The guests stay in fully equipped two and three-bedroom A-frame chalets. Programs include a six-night executive renewal and a 10-day weight-loss and fitness regimen. Facilities include a jacuzzi, sauna, health club, and indoor pool. Moderate. C-26, 108 Ranch, 100 Mile House, BC V0K 2E0. 604/791–5225.

**Sol Duc Hotspring Resort**—This rustic family resort on the Olympic Peninsula was built in 1910 and has been attracting families to its three-tiled 98-degree sulphur springs ever since. The 32 rustic cabins recently received a badly needed coat of paint. Too much renovation, the oldtimers say, would ruin its charm. Rates are moderate. Highway 101, between Port Angeles and Forks. P.O. Box 2169, Port Angeles, WA 98362. 206/327–3583.

## Wine and Food Weekends

**Steamboat Inn**—This excellent inn on the North Umpqua River in southern Oregon is famous as a fishing resort. Each winter and spring, though, the inn offers a series of food and wine weekends featuring chefs from outstanding Oregon restaurants, winemakers from area vineyards, and authors of cookbooks. Guests either stay in eight cozy cabins connected by a veranda or in four secluded cabins tucked away in the forest. Prices for the cabins are moderate, with a reasonable fee charged for the special weekend dinners. Steamboat, OR 97447–9703. 503/498–2411.

## Holiday Delights

**Empress Hotel**—Lovely on the outside and sometimes a bit time-worn on the inside, this majestic 488-room hotel recently underwent a much-needed face-lift. Christmas at the Empress is celebrated much like they did in the days of Empire, with a four-day package visit that includes an Imperial Dinner, musical entertainment, elaborate teas, and other delights. Stay over until New Year's and you can enjoy the Scottish Hogmanay, a celebration with a dinner, dance, Scottish dancers and pipers, and other diversions. Expensive. 721 Government Street, Victoria, BC V8W 1W5. 604/384–8111, 800/268–9411.

## *Life Aboard*

**MV Challenger**—Ever wanted to live aboard a tugboat? You can at the MV Challenger, a 96-foot tug built in 1944 for the Army and used as a working tug until 1981. It's now a bunk and breakfast tied up on Lake Union in Seattle. The tug offers seven staterooms (choose one of the four with a private bath). The best is the Captain's Cabin, a spacious two-room suite. The tug offers great views of the Seattle skyline and a different way to stay in the city. Moderate. 809 Fairview Place N, Seattle, WA 98109. 206/340–1201.

**Wharfside Bed & Breakfast**—The rooms at this B&B are in the *Jacquelyn*, a 60-foot sailboat tied up in Friday Harbor on San Juan Island. There are two rooms, one of which has a private half-bath. A stay here is charming, but we suggest you rent the entire boat (privacy is a very transient thing on boats of this size). That raises the rate for a one-night stay to the expensive category. P.O. Box 1212, Friday Harbor, San Juan Island, WA 98250. 206/378–5661.

Seattle's Pioneer Square hosts many festivals, and even the police get in the festive mood. *(Seattle-King County News Bureau)*

# CHAPTER 9

# *Festivals*

*T*he Pacific Northwest's calendar is crammed full of festivals celebrating the arts, history, cultural and ethnic heritage, and the great outdoors. Here is a list of the best of the festivals.

Dates change from year to year, so call the number listed or check with the local tourism officials for the current dates, times, and admission prices (if any).

## January

**Russian Christmas Celebration**—The Russian Orthodox Church in Sitka, Alaska, celebrates the holiday and its heritage. 907/747-8120.

**Chinese New Year**—Late January or early February, with parades, fireworks, displays, and other activities. The best festivals are held in Seattle (206/623-8171) and Vancouver, B.C. (604/683-2000).

## February

**Oregon Shakespeare Festival**—A busy schedule of contemporary plays and, during the prime summer months, three classics by the Bard, from February through October. 800/547-8052.

**Fat Tuesday**—Seattle's version of the Mardi Gras, with a parade, street concerts, and other activities in Pioneer Square. 206/682-4648.

**Festival of Native Arts**—This festival in Fairbanks celebrates the art, dance, and culture of Alaska's native people. 907/474-7181.

**Yukon Quest International Dogsled Race**—The race is from Whitehorse in Yukon Territory to Fairbanks. 403/667-6036.

**Northwest Flower and Garden Show**—Five acres of plants, flowers, and displays at the Washington State Convention and Trade Center in Seattle. 206/789-5333.

**Rain or Shine Dixieland Jazz Festival—**Presidents Day Weekend, when Aberdeen, Washington, celebrates with continuous concerts throughout the town. 206/533-2910.

## March

**Pacific Rim Whale Festival—**The migrating whales offshore are the center of a big festival at Pacific Rim National Park in Tofino, B.C. The festivities last from the last week in March into April. 604/725-3414.

**Iditarod Trail Sled Dog Race—**The big race in the land of ice and snow, covering more than 1,000 miles from Anchorage to Nome, Alaska. 907/376-5155.

**Winter Carnival—**Fairbanks celebrates with a week of dogsled races, dances, a parade, ice and snow-sculpting contests, arts and crafts, and music. 907/452-1105.

## April

**Daffodil Festival Grand Floral Parade—**A tradition for more than half a century in the Puyallup Valley, this huge parade visits all the valley's towns (Tacoma, Puyallup, Orting, and Sumner). 206/627-6176.

**International Wine Festival—**Biggest such event in Canada, with more than one hundred wineries from ten countries presenting their newest vintages at the Vancouver Trade and Convention Center. The festival lasts five days. 604/873-3311.

**Skagit Valley Tulip Festival—**Mount Vernon, Washington, comes alive with color when 1,500 acres of tulips bloom. 800/869-7107.

**Terrific Dixieland Jazz Festival—**Twenty bands from around the world play for five days in Victoria. 604/381-5277.

## May

**Hot Air Balloon Stampede—**Four days of ballooning, arts and crafts, a car show, and kite contest make this festival in Walla Walla, Washington, special. 206/525-0850.

**National Western Art Show and Auction**—More than one hundred rooms of paintings and sculpture for show and sale in Ellensburg, Washington. 509/962–2934.

**Northwest Folklife Festival**—Tens of thousands come to what is billed as the nation's largest celebration of folk art, music, dance, and food. It's in the Seattle Center over Memorial Day weekend. 206/684–7300.

**Seattle International Film Festival**—This 3 1/2-week-long festival brings films—good and bad, fine art and lowbrow, home-made and fancy foreign—to Seattle's theaters. 206/324–9996.

**Poulsbo Viking Fest**—The Olympic Peninsula town known as Little Norway celebrates its Viking heritage with dancing, music, a parade, and a lutefisk-eating (don't ask) contest. 206/779–4848.

**Rhododendron Festival**—The blossoming plants have almost become a sidelight to this big, busy festival of flowers, dog-and-owner runs, beard contests, tricycle races, and more. It's in Port Townsend, Washington. 206/385–2722.

**Slug Races**—Yeah, they are yucky, but what else is there to do in Old Town Florence, Oregon? 503/997–3128.

**Victorian Days**—People dress in costumes from a century ago, in a festival that includes antique cars, boat races, and other entertainment in Victoria, B.C. 604/382–2127.

**Washington State Apple Blossom Festival**—Eleven days of arts, crafts, food, music and, of course, apples in Wenatchee, Washington. 509/662–3616.

**Victoria Day**—National holiday in Canada on the next to last weekend in May.

## *June*

**Banff Festival of the Arts**—Opera, ballet, music, theater, visual arts, and readings at the Banff Centre from June through August. 403/762–3777.

**Peter Britt Festival**—Bluegrass, jazz, and classical music as well as ballet and musical theatre at this summer-long festival in Jacksonville, Oregon. 503/773–6077, 800/882–7488 (Western states only).

**Canadian International Dragonboat Festival**—Exotic boats race but don't miss the excellent Chinese food served at this Vancouver, B.C. celebration. 604/684–5151.

**Centrum Summer Arts Festival**—Three months (June through August) of music and art at Fort Worden State Park in Port Townsend, Washington. 206/385–3102.

**du Maurier Ltd. International Jazz Festival**—A newcomer to Vancouver, B.C., but already drawing almost one hundred jazz musicians from around the world for the two weeks of festivities. 604/682–0706.

**Mainly Mozart Festival**—The Seattle Symphony presents two weeks of tribute to Mozart and his contemporaries at the Meany Hall for the Performing Arts, University of Washington, Seattle. 206/443–4740.

**Rose Festival**—Thousands of roses, a parade, and a race by Indy-500-type cars highlight this 23-day celebration in Portland, Oregon. 503/228–9411.

**Umpqua Valley Arts Festival**—More than one hundred artisans present their creations in pottery, silk, jewelry, porcelain, and other media in Roseburg, Oregon. 503/672–2532.

**Sitka Summer Music Festival**—Three weeks of music ranging from pop to classical. 907/747–6774.

**International Pinot Noir Celebration**—Test the best of the Washington State pinot noirs. McMinnville. 503/472–4121.

## July

**Canada Day**—July 1, with celebrations throughout the provinces.

**Calgary Exhibition and Stampede**—It's known as a big rodeo, but the Stampede has square dancing, concerts, a parade, exhibition, stage shows, chuck wagon races, and a host of other activities. 403/261–0101.

**Edmonton's Klondike Days**—Raft and horse races, entertainment, a parade, and exhibits celebrate the Gold Rush days. 403/988–5455.

**Bellevue Jazz Festival**—The best jazz musicians in the Northwest play for three days on the third weekend in July at Central Park in Bellevue, Washington. 206/451–4106.

**Darrington Bluegrass Festival**—The small town of Darrington, Washington, in the Cascades foothills, comes alive with pickin' and dancin' on the third weekend in July. 206/436–1077.

**Folk Music Festival**—More than 200 performers, 12 cultures, and three days of fun at Jericho Park in British Columbia. 604/879–2931.

**Harrison Festival of the Arts**—Ten days of music, art, workshops, and lectures in this resort northeast of Vancouver, B.C. 604/796–3664.

**International Comedy Fest**—A laugh riot, lasting ten days, on Granville Island in Vancouver, B.C. 604/683–0883.

**Olympic Music Festival**—Take a barn on a peaceful farm on the Olympic Peninsula, bring in a top string quartet from some major city, and you have this nine-week festival in the town of Quilcene, Washington. 206/527–8839.

**Pacific Northwest Highland Games**—Celebrate your Scottish heritage, or at least your fake Scottish heritage, with games, music, foods, dances, and more in Enumclaw, Washington. 206/522–2874, 206/522–2541.

**San Juan Island Dixieland Jazz Festival**—Three days of live jazz at Friday Harbor. 206/378–5509.

**Seafair**—More than 40 years old, this festival has hydroplane races on Lake Washington, a Blue Angels air show, ethnic celebrations, a torchlight parade, and other fun activities through early August. 206/623–7000.

**Vancouver Folk Music Festival**—More than 200 performers from around the world perform at this festival in Jericho Beach Park in Vancouver, B.C., 604/879–2931.

## August

**Evergreen State Fair**—Eleven days of country music, rodeo, lumberjack contests, chili cookoffs, and car races in Monroe, Washington. 206/339–3309.

**Gig Harbor Jazz Festival**—You can drive or sail into this festival at Celebrations Meadow in Gig Harbor, Washington. 206/627-1504.

**Mount Hood Jazz Festival**—Great music and grand setting in Gresham, Oregon. 503/666-3810.

**Washington Food and Wine Festival**—Sample vintages from the Northwest wineries (or stomp a few grapes yourself) at this festival in Woodinville, Washington. 206/481-8300.

## September

**Pendleton Round-Up**—Major rodeo and Indian gathering at this week-long event in mid-September in eastern Oregon. 800/452-9403 in Oregon, 800/547-8911 outside the state.

**Bumbershoot**—Selected artisans join some big names in music for a huge arts festival over Labor Day weekend at the Seattle Center. 206/622-5123.

**International Film Festival**—It isn't Cannes, but you can view more than 125 films from more than 30 countries at this Vancouver, B.C., event. 604/685-0260.

## October

**Salmon Festival**—Salmon barbecues, arts and crafts, music, and other fun things highlight this annual event in Oxbow Park in Gresham, Oregon. 503/248-5050.

**Issaquah Salmon Days**—The return of the salmon is celebrated on the first weekend in October with a parade, music, dances, and food. 206/392-0661.

**Alaska Day Celebration**—This multiday event in Sitka on October 18 commemorates the transfer of Alaska from Russia to the United States. 907/747-8086.

## November

**Symphony of Trees**—Dozens of decorated trees go on display in Anchorage for this Anchorage Symphony fundraiser. 907/274-8668.

## December

**Christmas Lighting**—The Bavarian-theme town of Leavenworth, Washington, lights up for the holidays. Other activities include evening concerts. 206/548–5807.

**Whale Watch Week**—The official whale-watch counters need volunteers to help out in Newport, Oregon. 503/876–3011.

**First Night**—Just call it a smorgasbord of culture. For only a few dollars, you can enjoy all forms of cultural films, theater, and concerts at Vancouver's stages and halls on New Year's Eve. 604/669–9894.

# Index